THE WAR

REQUIEM

KAIA SOLVEIG

PREUS

THE WAR REQUIEM

KAIA SOLVEIG PREUS

ESSAY PRESS

2020

A WINNER OF THE 2018 ESSAY PRESS + UNIVERSITY OF WASHINGTON BOTHELL
MFA IN CREATIVE WRITING & POETICS BOOK CONTEST

SELECTED BY REBECCA BROWN

ISBN 978-1-7344984-0-0

Printed and bound in the United States by Versa Press, Inc.
Cover and book design by Travis Sharp
Cover image by Robert Couse-Baker and used in accordance with Creative Commons CCBY
Author photo by ell film

Essay Press is a non-profit organization dedicated to publishing innovative, explorative, and culturally relevant prose.
essaypress.org

This book is made possible by the financial support of the University of Washington Bothell MFA in Creative Writing and Poetics.
uwb.edu/mfa

Distributed by Small Press Distribution
1341 Seventh Street
Berkeley, California 94710
spdbooks.org

10 9 8 7 6 5 4 3 2

EP BOOK #106

CONTENTS

IN MEMORY OF

Paul Preus

Solveig Preus

&

Niecy Byrd Culbertson

INTRODUCTION

THIS IS A book about falling in love with art. It's a book about being drawn to a piece of music and then getting to live with it then with others with it and where it came from and where it can take you. It's about how art is beyond us, transcendent, but also inside us, visceral, the thing most in and of us and the world. It's about how art can help the world. About how art can help ease the pain of war and wrong and be like a cry of grief or hope.

The *War Requiem* was written by a pacifist. Let me rephrase that: the first *War Requiem*, a piece of music, was written by Benjamin Britten, a man who didn't want to fight in World War II when almost everyone else in England did, and one of the most important composers of the 20th century and also gay person who, years before Stonewall, composed much of his music to be sung by his life partner, the tenor Peter Pears. After World War II, Britten was commissioned to write something for the reconsecration, in 1962, of the Coventry Cathedral, the 14th century original having been destroyed by enemy bombing. Britten's *Requiem* is a mash-up of the Latin Mass for the Dead and poems by Wilfred Owen, a British poet who died in the first World War. Britten's work is dedicated to several soldiers who died during World War II or shortly thereafter due to suicide or other effects of war.

The second *War Requiem* was written by a 21st century American woman, Kaia Solveig Preus. I have no idea if Preus is a pacifist, but I do know that she is a writer who gets how art can live in the world. How it lives first in history, in the context of its making, then lives in you, in how you come across it and when you do, then how it lives in your history too, and in how you learn that it's made by people who have lives and losses and obsessions not so different from your own. How art and artists speak to each other across time and between countries and genders and media, sometimes alone but sometimes with one or more in a room or on a stage or concert hall, finding each other and listening and passing on how we try to live with each other in our beautiful difficult world. Sometimes art is what gets us through war or whatever war-like thing we're embroiled in.

Preus tells us about learning the hard work and discipline then ecstasy of singing the *War Requiem* with others. Then learning about Britten and Pears, then Britten and Owen, their lives and wars in a mash-up with hers because history and biography sing in call-and-response with memory and memoir as they show us where we're from and how we're like.

Art is not an alternative to the world. Art is not an escape from, not a solution to the world. Art is the world.

The *War Requiem*s (Britten's music and Preus' book) remind us art can renovate the world.

—Rebecca Brown

THIS PAGE IS a staff. These words, musical notes. Periods, commas, question marks, and, of course, the dashes—rests. I close my eyes and listen. My part will become clear.

Again, again an interruption in the *War Requiem*. A motif cuts in. It's from—where? You don't remember the movement, but you remember the feeling. Brass fanfare: the inevitable, false triumph of war. The glint of harp: hope despite everything. Even the single quarter note of the timpani, a distant explosion, the muffled beat of your own heart. Timpani—every time, you feel the hollow death of a note passing through you, ending.

Pay attention, I tell myself. Be alert. But do not struggle to grasp onto everything. All you need to understand is what you sing right now.

1. REQUIEM AETERNAM

"Et lux perpetua luce et eis."

"Let the perpetual light shine upon them."

THOUGH IT HAS been years since I sang the *War Requiem*, the music won't let me go. I listen to the piece as I drive to and from my graduate classes, work, and the library. The brass fanfare in the second movement stops my heart each time—I gasp, feel a sour buzzing just behind my ears, and blink out tears that seem to wait behind my eyes for specifically this moment. How, I wonder, how can those four notes, played by an instrument I've never even touched, affect me every time I hear it? I wait for the effect to wear off, but I hit repeat and hit repeat and fireworks explode inside again.

I change lanes and I sing the soprano's high notes in the *Lacrimosa*. I pass cars and semis and I swing my head with the timpani as if watching the sky for explosions in the distance or incoming cannonballs. When I park, I often stay in my car to finish the movement. Shutting the car door in the middle of the piece seems unholy, somehow.

As I listen to the *War Requiem* each day, I start asking it questions. Why does the choir repeat this section in a hushed *pianissimo*? What do these Latin words mean, exactly, these words that accompany such haunting sections of music? Who is this soprano singing the *Lacrimosa* and how does her voice have so much control across large intervals?

In between classes and work, I start researching the *War Requiem* online, but reading about the composer and the poet whose words lend themselves to the score isn't enough. I want to hear their voices.

One day, I go to the library to pick up two collections of letters I've ordered, one of the composer Benjamin Britten, and one of the soldier poet Wilfred Owen. I tell the woman at the front desk my name and she searches the shelves behind her. She bends down to retrieve the books and when she turns around with one in each hand, I see that they are enormous. Both must be at least five hundred pages. She sets them down on the counter with a thud, and I hand her my library card. I do not know whether I should feel proud or embarrassed of checking out such huge books. I carry them to my car.

I bring the books into my little house, set them down on the kitchen table, and start paging through them. The letters' dates seem so distant; the very first letters Wilfred Owen wrote are from 1899. As I look over the letters, I start to wonder: Who am I to imagine the lives of these two men—one a soldier and poet, the other a world-famous composer? I have so little in common with them. I don't know very much about their art and I know barely anything about the time periods in which they lived. All I did was request these books from the library, and now here they are: two lives in letters.

I close the books and rest my hands on the covers. Who am I to read these?

I want to understand the *War Requiem* and the people responsible for the joy and terror and awe I feel every time I sing or hear it. I decide that is reason enough for me to read these books. I look at the names stamped in gold: Wilfred Owen on the green book, Benjamin Britten on the black. This moment feels sacred to me. This moment feels like the start of something.

BENJAMIN BRITTEN TAKES his first breath on the Feast Day of St. Cecilia, the patron saint of music. He grows up in the fishing port of Lowestoft where salty winds whip through the quaint town and fill his ears with the roar and slap of waves along the coast. From early on, his mother, Edith, grooms him to join the ranks of the great "B" composers: Beethoven, Brahms, and Bach. Britten senses from a young age that his father doesn't believe he can make it as a musician, but this doesn't bother him. While other children his age run to the piers jutting into the North Sea, Britten stays close to his family piano and the sheet music his mother keeps in tall stacks. He is fascinated by the appearance of music on the page. The dots and dashes and lines create beautiful patterns and images that somehow turn into sound. He loves the way music enters his body and makes his mind see memories, his chest contract with emotion, his hands tingle as if they, too, want to pick up an instrument and join in the conversation. How could flat markings on a page become something invisible that made him feel so much?

To him, there is no question. Music lives inside of him.

THROUGHOUT HIS CHILDHOOD in Shrewsbury, Wilfred Owen would play with his three siblings and sometimes even dress up as a priest to amuse his mother, Susan, but in his teenage years, he becomes withdrawn. He spends his time cradling beloved books in his slender hands. He falls in love with Keats most of all. Shelley, Tennyson, Wilde, and Swinburne, too. His mother wants him to make his play-acting real and enter the church, but Owen has the stirrings of poetry inside. He loves the music in the lines, the beauty and richness in the images depicting the world around him. He is destined to be a poet. He knows it.

Owen doesn't play sports. He doesn't engage in family activities. His father scowls at him, but Owen ignores this. He reads. He flips pages with shaking fingers. He ingests the words, whispers them to himself even after he has closed the book. He dreams of leaving Shrewsbury to attend the University of London and study the great Romantics with scholars and like-minded students.

He tries his hand at writing. At times he writes furiously, at others with a pensive calm. He crosses out line after line and starts again. Ink stains his fingers. He doesn't know if what he writes is any good, but he keeps going—he can't help but move the pen across the page, create inked waves from his *t*s and *m*s and *r*s.

His father grows exasperated. There isn't any money, he tells Owen, who watches his father's face turn red with frustration, embarrassment. There won't be any university, he hears his father say. Owen looks at him and nods, and then turns back to his paper and pen. Later, when his father's pronouncement still clangs in his ears, in his heart, he turns to his beloved Keats and reads, "Bright star, would I were stedfast as thou art…"

WHEN I FIRST considered auditioning for choir at college, my mother told me of her days singing in one of her college's choirs. During her first year of choir, she sat beside a senior music major with the most beautiful voice she had ever heard. This senior had auditioned for their school's most prestigious ensemble, but she did not get in. My mother always told me that the key to choir is blending. The senior who sat next to her had a beautiful voice, yes, but it was a solo voice, more suited to opera than to choral music. When singing with a choir, if one voice stands out more than the others, the entire group sounds unbalanced. The audience will grow distracted from the music and try to find the outlier. If, for example, one person sings an "eh" in the second syllable of "forever" instead of a schwa (similar to the "eu" sound as in the French for "peu"), the entire one-hundred-voice ensemble sounds flat and appears tired and unrehearsed. Singing in a choir is all about listening, tuning, blending. It is about hearing the singers on either side of you and across the risers from you above hearing yourself. It is an act of humility.

AS THE YOUNGEST of four children, Benjamin Britten often plays alone. He runs up and down the beach near his house. He draws pictures in the wet sand with sticks and bits of driftwood. He crouches at the place where water meets earth and watches minnows and hermit crabs swim and walk and live. He wonders at the worlds on the other sides of the sea he knows so well. Is there another little boy like him watching hermit crabs at his own edge of ocean and sand? He reaches into the cool water and picks a hermit crab up by its shell. The crab recoils and Britten sets it in his palm, waits and watches as the crab's legs, then claws, then stemmed eyes slowly emerge from the mossy shell. The crab is so small and the ocean floor stretches wider and deeper than Britten can imagine. Gently, he drops the crab back into the sea and he leans back on his heels, his arms wrapped around his shins. He watches the crab scuttle away. Gentle waves touch his toes. He is small, too.

AT THE URGING of his mother and the Reverend Herbert Wigan, Owen leaves for Dunsden in the fall of 1911 to study at the vicarage. At eighteen years old, he is not convinced that a religious life is for him, but studying under the vicar will provide more educational opportunities, and, more importantly, will give him time and space away from his family to focus on poetry.

Owen attends the church services—sometimes as many as six in a day—and visits the poor living in cramped cottages nearby. He returns to the vicarage after long days praying with the sick and downtrodden to see Reverend Wigan feasting on dishes prepared by a multitude of servants. Owen doesn't see how the church's doctrines and doings help the ordinary people beyond the church doors who search for solace and hope.

At night, he retires to his books and finds comfort there. The words feel holy in a way that this life in the vicarage does not. He reads his favorite poems over and over again, lodging them in his chest, hoping that some of them will mingle and rearrange and bloom as poems of his own.

AT THE END of my freshman year of college, I auditioned for St. Olaf's Chapel Choir. I prepared thirty-two bars of a hymn my mother taught me: "How Brightly Beams the Morning Star." I knew that I'd be asked to sight-read and to sing one of the school's favorite hymns, "Beautiful Savior," a cappella. In the weeks leading up to the ten-minute audition, I hummed vocal exercises while I walked to and from classes and I practiced sight-reading out of a hymn book I nicked from the chapel. I tucked myself into the small practice rooms that sat in the basements of many dorms and barricaded the glass doors with my backpack and books. I sang while stretching my arms up toward the ceiling. I filled my world with sound.

BRITTEN BEGINS COMPOSING in earnest. At seven years old, he hands his mother a piece of paper covered with musical notes and lyrics. Dutifully, she takes the composition to the piano and young Britten watches her attempt to play it. Her face looks puzzled and when she plunks the notes on the piano, they sound wrong. The key and time signatures don't match the notes, and the vocal and accompaniment lines don't match each other, but he has written it down. It is a composition.

COUGHING FITS RATTLE Owen's bones. His fever will not break. His limbs ache. A winter draft creeps in through the thin glass of the vicarage window. His mother would tell him to pray. The vicar would tell him to pray. Owen cannot pray. Coughs shudder through a body that feels not his own. He shivers beneath his blankets and looks to the white ceiling. He will never be able to attend university. Somehow, he knows this now. His dreams of becoming a poet recede further from him, yet he will not let them go. He coughs again and feels as if his lungs are made of cracking glass. He closes his eyes. He gives himself to sleep.

　　Owen wakes in the night. Darkness all around him. A cold sweat slicks his skin. He has had the dream again. In it, a pale and drawn face floats in a pool of black water. The dark eyes stare straight up and are empty. They seem to fall toward the back of his skull, a dark well deepening forever. There is no question that the young man is dead. There is no question that the face is his own.

THE DAY OF the audition, I locked myself into a practice room a half hour before my time slot. I warmed up as my voice teacher, Margaret, taught me: lip trills, hums, soft scales on a full breath. With sweaty palms and shaking fingers, I played chord progressions on the piano as I worked up the scale with my voice. As a first soprano, I knew the choir director, Dr. A, would ask me to jump up on high exercises. Competition for a first soprano spot is typically fierce in the choral world. Because high notes tend to be heard more easily than lower ones, a choir needed fewer first sopranos than any other vocal part. I had never seen a St. Olaf choir program with more than twelve first sopranos. At the thought, my stomach clenched. I willed myself to breathe deeply and focus on how far I'd come in the music world after just one year at St. Olaf.

When I started taking voice lessons in junior high, I thought that sound just came from my mouth and the small muscles in my throat called vocal chords. By singing in my high school's choir, I learned the importance of breath, of the diaphragm. But it wasn't until I started taking voice lessons at the collegiate level every week from Margaret that I realized the full depth of knowledge and awareness required to vocalize properly. True, breath and vocal chords did matter, but they were just the surface layer. Singing required a hyper-awareness of the body at the same time it needed a release from tightness and stress. Everything mattered. The position of my feet, the bend in my knees, the straightness of my back, the placement of my skull above my spine. Even the position of my hands and the tension they might hold.

I looked at my blurry reflection in the glass door of the practice room. I lifted my chin and imagined roots pulling my feet straight down into the ground. I remembered a voice lesson I'd had only a few weeks before. In it, Margaret and I practiced standing correctly for a full twenty minutes. I stood like a bent-kneed marionette: wooden and waiting for some larger being to jerk my voice into movement. When I sang, my voice came out reedy, breathy. "Okay, that's not working," Margaret said. She had me sing while holding a blow-up exercise ball above my head. "Better," she said. "Now, throw it up and down."

I looked around the room at the statues of angels and Buddhas and the lamps made of paper.

"It's okay, don't worry about the stuff. Throw it! Bend your knees. Let your stomach relax. Don't worry about being fat! Forget about the rules." I tossed the ball above my head and sang *Hung-ahhhh* on a descending scale. "Good! Good," Margaret said. "Linger on the *ng*, feel how that opens the cathedral inside your mouth. Let your tongue drop. Think of a dog tongue all loose and floppy, relax, relax!" Her gray curls shook around her head as she yelled to me. "Do you see how the *ng* sound creates space in the back of your throat? You're giving the sound more room for resonance." She had me do this for about ten minutes. I stopped listening to myself and only focused on my tongue moving up and down, a drawbridge to sound. "Now try without the ball."

I set down the ball and imagined the fluid in my knees cradling my entire body. I kept my body soft, but my diaphragm engaged. I pictured my head floating above my spine. I was a life-sized bobblehead, a vessel for sound. I took a breath and visualized the air going down to my thighs. I opened the dome of my mouth and let the sound come out. *Hung-ahhhh.* My notes pierced through the breath and came out clear. The mask of my face buzzed, resonant and full of sound.

"All right," Margaret said. "Now we're getting somewhere." She nodded, looked at her bright green wristwatch. "I'll see you next week."

Now, I hoped that I could access that same sound in my audition that I'd found while working with Margaret. I was so nervous, though, and nerves would only tighten up my body and my voice. I checked the time on my phone. I had about five minutes. It was time to go. Taking deep breaths, I packed up my backpack and walked to Dr. A's office.

In the fall of 1921, Britten goes to his first day at South Lodge School for Boys in Lowestoft. He puts on his knee socks and his best pair of shoes. He tries to tuck his curly hair beneath the school-issued cap. South Lodge is not far from his home, but he still feels excited. He will make new friends, read long and challenging books, and play sports with the other boys.

Early on in the day, Britten walks amongst the other students in the dark and crowded hallway toward his next class. Before he reaches the door, he hears the sound of a boy being beaten from a nearby office. He listens to a crack and then a boy crying out. Around him, the students walk on as if they have heard nothing. Britten stops walking. All the other sounds of the school building—boys talking, shoes squeaking on the floor, doors opening and closing—fade away. All Britten can hear is the crack and cry of both beater and beaten. Why is nobody rushing to the boy's aid? What did he do to deserve this punishment? Is any action bad enough to justify violence?

The rest of the boys in the hall disappear into their respective classrooms, but Britten doesn't notice, even when he is left alone in the hall. All he can do is listen to the crack and cry, the crack and cry, the cry, cry, cry.

I BREATHED AND held my head up while walking to Dr. A's office, hoping that my feigned confidence would become real. This would be the first time that Dr. A had ever heard my voice alone. I had seen him from across the orchestra during Christmas Festival performances that winter. He conducted all of the choirs together for the "Sanctus (Requiem)" by Maurice Duruflé. I stood in the second row with the rest of the first-year women's choir, singing the high notes as quietly as I could. The song was beautiful, and I was mesmerized by Dr. A's confident flicks of the baton as he raised his eyebrows, leaned toward us, and pulled our truest sounds out of our throats. He was a magician to me. An artist. A perfect listener. When I thought of singing in front of him, my shoulders tightened with anxiety.

Dr. A was young and had spiky blond hair, a ruddy Norwegian complexion, and a range that covered bass to first soprano. I had heard him in Christmas Fest rehearsals singing the first soprano parts in falsetto to demonstrate a point. Along with the other freshmen girls, I had swooned at this.

I ran a hand through my hair and set my backpack on the chair outside his office door. I wanted to impress him. I wanted to be in his choir, Chapel Choir, the choir that was known for its heart. I pushed my shoulders back, fixed a nervous smile on my face, and knocked.

Almost instantly, Dr. A opened the door and smiled. "Hello, welcome!" His tenor voice rang clear and full even in speech. He seemed excited to see me—he acted as though I was already his friend, not some freshman he had never met. I felt myself blush and dragged my hands through my hair, pulling it into a quick ponytail while I followed him into the bright office. A grand piano sat in the corner. There was an exercise ball instead of a chair rolled beneath the desk.

He told me to stand wherever I liked and then had me sing a few easy warm ups to get a sense of my voice. I kept my knees bent and moved my hands in fluid motions at my waist while I focused on using my breath to power my voice up and over the note, soaring through the descending scale. Things felt easy and relaxed in my throat and the tone sounded clear enough to me, so I stopped worrying and just let myself sing. Dr. A nodded while I sang, and I took this as a good sign. He appeared happy to hear my voice.

"First soprano," he said, and I smiled. "Now, what hymn did you bring?"

I unfolded a xeroxed copy of the hymn my mother had taught me over spring break. I placed it on the music stand and asked for an F. "How brightly beams the morning star / What sudden radiance from afar / Doth cheer us with its shining." The hymn showed the range of my voice, and I enjoyed singing it. I smiled as I sang.

When I finished, I stumbled through a short sight-reading exercise and then Dr. A asked me to sing the chorus of "Beautiful Savior," the hymn all of the choirs had sung just a few months ago at the close of our Christmas Festival. Afterward, he thanked me and I thanked him and then I left. I had sung my best. There was nothing more I could do.

Britten takes music lessons with renowned composers while he attends South Lodge. He lives two lives: one of music and beauty, the other ugly, unjust. At night he attends concerts in Norwich: Mahler and Bridge, Shostakovich and Stravinsky. He closes his eyes in the concert hall and listens to the orchestra. The music feeds something in him—he feels peaceful and exhilarated at once.

When he returns to school each day, he shrinks in his desk when the headmaster strikes other boys for misbehaving. Later, he stands on the sides of the schoolyard and watches the boys pummel each other. They kick and punch and bleed. They scream and snarl, their mouths backlit by blood, their teeth stained pink. A quiet fury, a deep unrest, bubbles beneath Britten's skin. He does not intervene, but sits away from them, watching, breathing, watching.

OWEN DREAMS AGAIN. This time only his empty hand floats in the black water. He does not know if his body is beneath the surface or not.

There is not enough time. Owen wants to be a poet more than anything, but doubt shadows his every thought. He believes in the power of words on paper, but he struggles to believe that he, too, can contribute to the world of words, the twenty-six letters that arrange and rearrange, create miracles.

A WEEK AFTER my audition, I walked into the music building alone. An eight-foot tall bulletin board stood near the front entrance, covered in flapping brochures and fliers pinned to the cork. Stapled tight in the center of the board, the lists of the new choir members waited for all the choir hopefuls. My friends and I had heard that over two hundred students tried out for Chapel Choir alone. As a first soprano, I auditioned for one of ten spots, tops.

I stepped up to the board, my heart in my throat, my hands clenched in clammy fists. I passed over the lists of the St. Olaf Choir, Cantorei, Manitou, and Viking. There—Chapel Choir—First Sopranos—I searched the short list and found it. Kaia Preus. One of eight first sopranos. A shimmering breath rushed into my throat. I'd made it.

IN 1927, BRITTEN'S viola teacher introduces him to composer Frank Bridge. Lessons with Mr. Bridge are grueling and frustrating. Britten often leaves in tears from exhaustion at the sheer force of concentration Bridge expects him to maintain throughout the three, sometimes four-hour lessons. He is fourteen years old.

Today is one of Britten's first lessons with Mr. Bridge. Britten brings a composition and Bridge holds the paper in his hand, studies it carefully, his long hair hanging forward onto the page. "Get up," Bridge says. "Go stand over there. Listen." Bridge sits at the piano and plays the composition. "Is this really what you meant?" He turns and stares at Britten who stands in the corner at the other side of the room.

Britten feels like shrinking. "No," he says.

Bridge nods almost imperceptibly. Britten can't decode the thoughts behind Bridge's eyes, but they can't be all bad, he reasons, because he wouldn't be here if Bridge didn't think there was something in him that could do this. Britten walks back toward the piano and his teacher. It wasn't what he meant. He will try again.

OWEN LEAVES THE vicarage in 1913, religion now hollow to him. All he can think of is his poetry. He cannot attend university and he does not want to return home. He decides to go to France.

In Bordeaux, he spends much of his days teaching English to the children of a local family, but the majority of his thoughts go to poetry. Though he still feels the strain of self-doubt, he tries to work through it, returning to his paper and pen again and again. When the lines don't come willingly, he goes outside and lifts his face toward the warm sun. He walks among wildflowers and crouches down to see toads hopping about the grass. The afternoons are long and rich with the sound of rustling leaves, chirping birds, and humming insects. Here, outside in France, with poetry unfurling inside him, Owen feels happy. Perhaps the happiest he's ever been.

ON THE FIRST day of the 2013 spring semester, my last semester of college and of Chapel Choir, it was snowing and cold and would be for many months to follow. We knocked the snow off our boots and tennis shoes when we entered the glowing music building. We swung our backpacks and bags to the floor behind the risers and then we walked to our seats while Prince's "Let's Go Crazy" played on the surround sound. Dancing, squeaking along, we took our seats by our friends and asked each other about our winter breaks. Dr. A was nodding his head to the music while paging through a giant score sitting atop the grand piano. The *War Requiem*, we knew. I was supposed to have listened to a recording over break, but I was lazy and didn't. I had never heard the *War Requiem*. I had no idea what to expect. Two years before, when I had been a sophomore in my first year of Chapel Choir, we sang Brahms's *Ein deutsches Requiem*, which had been a beautiful and shimmering experience. I'd left each rehearsal with glistening eyes and soaring melodies still hovering in my throat. I figured this requiem would be somewhat like that.

At 3:10 p.m., Dr. A turned off the music and stood before us, smiling. "Welcome back," he said. Around me, shoulders relaxed and smiles peeked over scarves and winter sweaters. Here, more than anywhere else on campus, we felt comfortable. "We have a huge semester ahead of us, and I am so excited to work with you on Benjamin Britten's *War Requiem*."

He passed out the choral scores—thick white books—and we wrote our names in pencil on the inside cover. I paged through mine—it appeared to have belonged to both a soprano and a bass in past years. Those ghost students' markings circled and scratched the top and bottom staves. I turned to the music itself and focused on the notes and time signatures stamped in strong black ink. I felt my jaw clench and my fingers tighten on the score's edges. I couldn't tell if two notes next to each other were the same or if they were a third apart. Sharps, flats, and naturals floated beside almost every note like crooked black eyes. The notes looked heavy and beaten down. I felt that way, too, before I had sung even one note.

Dr. A had us turn to the first page of the first movement. "I'm going to play this first section for you. This is from the original recording with the Bach Choir and the London Symphony Orchestra." He stood at the piano and aimed the remote at the speakers. The music started quietly; the choir came in so subtly I barely heard it. I looked over my score to see Dr. A standing with his feet apart, conducting an invisible orchestra with an imaginary baton. For him to practice in front of us meant that this piece would elude perfection, maybe even for Dr. A. When the first section of the movement ended, Dr. A clicked it off and turned to the piano. "All right, your turn. Let's fright-scream." Fright-scream was his word for sight-read. We laughed and felt braver as we started charging through our mistakes.

The beginning was boring and hard. We stayed on one almost silent note for a long time. To blend while quiet and still maintain movement within a phrase—that was hard work. After a few times through, I took off my scarf and planted my feet a little wider apart.

When we jumped up intervals and octaves, I screeched along with the other sopranos, struggling to sustain notes that did not in any way mesh harmonically with the notes that the other parts tried to sing. Dr. A had us hold a chord all together and told us, "That's it. That's right." We could hardly believe him. This sounded wrong. Completely, totally wrong. Our ears had been trained by years of listening to hear harmonic, tonal sounds. This—this was the sound of unease incarnate. I used the back of one hand to wipe the sweat from my hairline. I stared at the score in my hand and imagined chucking it across the room. Dr. A expected us to learn this entire requiem in two and a half months? Less than half of us were music majors. There was no way I could read this.

The *War Requiem* made no sense to me. Threads upon threads wove themselves together, mirrored each other, played hide-and-seek. We couldn't keep up. We rehearsed and rehearsed and still could not remember which fugue came first, which diminuendo faded into nothing and which simply faded. The Latin stuck in our mouths like peanut butter. We flipped pages and missed entrances.

Yet, the precision of the piece astounded me. I listened to Dr. A affirm Britten's marking in the text again and again: "I cannot give you every entrance," he said. "I will do my best, but you must practice, must read your music, look at and trust your score."

I looked and I wondered: how could chaos be so certain?

IT IS THE end of a hot summer in 1914 and England has declared war on Germany. Owen doesn't know what this means for his homeland, for his family, or for his poetry. In dreams, he hears the boom of cannons and the staccato of guns. Owen sits in his room in Bordeaux with his head in his hands. He refuses to be dragged along with the other young, able-bodied men who enlist because it is the popular thing to do. On the other hand, if he refuses to enlist, he will be seen as a coward. He doesn't want to fight, but he also doesn't want to sit at home while other men die for their country and their families. He runs his hands through his hair and sits up and looks out the window. The sun falls through the glass in soft lines that look like butter against the white walls.

Owen stands and walks to his desk, riffles the pages of poetry he has written while in France. These beautiful words, this beautiful form— poetry. His greatest passion, his dream. What will happen to these words—English words—because of war?

He returns to England and enlists. He receives his uniform, a French phrase book, a tin of Bully Beef, and a pay book, the last page of which is reserved for a will and testament.

EVERY DAY, I go back. I close my eyes and visit again the last time my choir performed the *War Requiem*. Sunlight fell through the chapel's stained glass windows and dappled the audience in soft pinks and blues. Our conductor stood before us in his tuxedo. Before the first movement, his baton waited, stiff and still, in his hands. He took a breath, and so did I. The lights shone brightly on us and the audience faded from my vision. The conductor raised his hand and we entered the music.

Timpani, deep strings, a glint of chimes, then voices—one voice— floating, barely audible, from far away. The strings played across large intervals and the timing sounded off balance, somehow—the stress was on the first note, but the second was held longer, a five-four time signature worked into something new and strange. Then again, a stillness, a sureness, wound itself tightly inside each note. I held the score and I felt the importance of the paper, the weight of what it carried in ink, the portal contained in every marking. The strings continued to crescendo steadily, the intervals came closer together in note and time, and then the choir opened a valley of sound again. The chimes clanged louder, the percussion snapped in, and the brass section asserted itself, making the tritone's dissonance overt, challenging even.

As part of the chorus, I listened for the chimes. The chimes often served as our signal and we strained to hear them and to hear them accurately amidst everything else. Before me: heads of other sopranos, a full orchestra, a chamber orchestra, three soloists. Behind me: more choir members and organ pipes large enough to crawl inside. All of these sections, all of the instruments and musicians, would not come together until the final movement of the piece. Until then, the parts remained fractured: the orchestra, choir, and soprano soloist worked as one unit. The chamber orchestra and the tenor and baritone soloists, another. The children's choir and the smaller organ, yet another. The large organ would not come in until the final movement. Everything hung in the balance—everything strained to connect until the end was reached. Friction. Never had I heard so much friction in a piece of music.

The chimes rang out a tritone—F# and C, dissonant, close enough to belong together, but far enough apart to sound estranged. We oriented ourselves in this nebulous in-between. The F#-C tritone carried the piece and served as the most regularly occurring motif. After months of rehearsal, we understood it better now, this friction, this unrest. We let ourselves fall into it, trust it. The first movement was ending: the chimes rang out. We filled our insides with air and came in on a quiet breath. *Kyrie eleison, Christe eleison, Kyrie eleison. Lord, have mercy upon them, Christ have mercy upon them, Lord have mercy upon them.* I sang so quietly I could not hear my voice, the breath that carried my notes, a whisper. My heart banged against my ribs and I pressed a hand to my sternum, tried to press it back in—surely, the singers next to me could hear it, could feel it. I didn't know for sure, but I thought I had stopped singing. My breath had run out. All I was, now, was a beating heart, a shaking body held up by the thin notes around me. I trusted them. My lips still moved and I listened to my friends sing next to me—far away, strange.

We were angels. We sang for the dead.

2. DIES IRAE

"Dies irae, dies illa, solvet saeclum in favilla."

"This day, this day of wrath, shall consume the world in ashes."

THESE DAYS, I no longer wake up to the blue skies and cornfields of my college years. I don't sing in a choir anymore. Instead, I practice arias and art songs while I dump rice into a pot or flip frozen veggie burgers in a pan in my little house in Virginia. I hum my own simple compositions as I walk down the driveway to get the mail, and I sing along to the violin melodies on the classical radio station when I drive to work. I live alone in a small cottage with a slanted floor and a sagging ceiling. From my kitchen table, I can lean toward the window and see hawks flying above the tall trees that surround my home.

I sing to myself, loose and easy. I fill my kitchen with sound. Sometimes I will be washing dishes, singing the *Lacrimosa*, Latin words that I swore I'd never learn, and I will close my eyes. In my mind, I watch the mountains lift and stretch themselves flat. I stand straight on risers, not crooked on the slanted floor. When I sing, my voice is not alone any longer; the sounds of my surrounding friends make me brave, and I sing louder. I forget the soapy dishes in my hands.

A LETTER FROM his mother. In the dying light of day, Owen sits outside his assigned hut in Hare Hall Camp in Essex and turns the thin paper toward the disappearing sun. He reads of his family's goings-on at home, the results of his little brother's school tests. In the curl and loop of her *h*s and *l*s, Owen imagines his mother's arms wrapping around him in an embrace.

In the wave of the *s*, her hands, smooth and pink, brush his hair away from his face.

All day, Owen branded blisters on his palms, digging trenches. He cut into the earth with his shovel, and moved dirt into mountains. Now, he relishes the letter his mother sent him and reads it over and over until the evening's last light fades into night. Then he tucks the letter in with his belongings and goes to sit around the fire with the other young men he's come to know these weeks in various English camps. He slides a piece of bread onto the end of his bayonet and holds it over the burning logs. What will it be like to pierce flesh? How much will the skin and muscle resist before the bayonet punctures a liver, a heart, a hard part of bone? He shivers. The fire burns hot.

THE WORLD COMES to life around Britten after he graduates from the Royal College of Music. Everywhere he looks, colors seem brighter and smiles from friends and acquaintances dazzle him. His music is making its way into the world. Since graduating college, *Sinfonietta*, Op. 1, *Simple Symphony*, Op. 4, and a quartet have been performed in concert halls in London and Suffolk, his home. The BBC broadcasts some of the recordings, and Britten reads reviews in *The Times*, which range in praise and critique.

What Britten writes is confusing. His music takes on multiple layers and goes through major transformations within the arc of a piece. He often chooses to set complex poems that audience members strain to make out over the orchestration in expansive concert halls.

After rehearsals, he goes home to a boarding house full of middle-aged women and bends over his journal, scratching out his disappointment at the musicians' failings. How his music is received depends largely upon the talents and techniques of the musicians. As a first-rate viola player himself, he demands nothing less than perfection. Even frustrated musicians, ambivalent listeners, and harsh critics shake their heads in awe at the thought of how incredibly young he is: just twenty-two, with a life full of music and creation before him.

AFTER A YEAR of training to be an officer, the military ships Owen to France. He pulls at the damp sheets in his tent and tries to tuck them into something resembling a bed. He and his tentmate begged the doctor for two stretchers upon which to sleep, and while not comfortable, it is better than being directly on the mud. Always, always mud. Mud in his pajamas, in his bed, in his shoes. He doesn't remember what being dry feels like. Owen is terrified that his feet will become like some of the other men's: black and green and purple, like rotten fruit. He doesn't know how they continue to walk on such feet. Their skin disintegrates, their bones threaten to puncture the blackened surface and still, the men walk on. When a soldier in his company receives a pair of socks, it always goes to the man whose own are in the worst state.

Owen tugs the sheets tighter around the stretcher, and that's when he hears them: gun shots. His first since arriving in France. At the *rat-a-tat-tat* he thinks he sees the candle flame jump in time with his nerves. A few seconds pass and the flame relaxes, grows fatter near the wick, and Owen fills his lungs with air.

BRITTEN FLIES TO Barcelona in 1936 where a friend from the Royal College of Music, Antonio Brosa, will join him in a performance of his Suite, for violin and piano, Op. 6. While in Barcelona, Britten sees the sights and enjoys the weather, and he also attends the first performance of a violin concerto composed by the recently deceased Alban Berg. Though he had never met Berg, Britten reveres his compositions. The world of composing is incredibly small and he feels the loss of another artist acutely. In their own ways, they are all trying to make the world more beautiful out of black notes on white paper, the communion of sounds made by people working together toward creation.

Hearing Berg's music at the concert drenches Britten in awe and anger at losing such a talent. When the applause ends after the concert, he stands with the crowd and moves swiftly out into the night. He needs to sit at a desk and take out his pencil, mark paper with strong lines and sure ovals. He needs to do what he can—no matter how much or how little—to make meaning out of this confusing and unfair world. A life cannot last. Music can.

DAMP SPOTS APPEARED on the score beneath my thumbs. Even my fingers were sweating and my feet felt hot. I glanced toward the clock. 3:45. I still had thirty minutes of this. Dr. A had been working with the tenors, but now he turned his attention to the altos and sopranos. "Rehearsal score twenty-one," he said. I rocked onto the outsides of my rubber soles and watched the old fabric on my shoes gape into holes like jagged mouths. "All right, let's hit it," said Dr. A. He punched his fingers on the piano, giving us a fresh listen at the key. This section of the movement was in 7/4 time and he softly counted us in and then took a sharp breath on the seven.

We entered. *Tu. Ba. Mi. Rum. Spar. Gens. So. Num.* We sounded like a car jerking backward and forward.

"Stop." Dr. A held up his hand and we fell silent. "Don't let the quarter rests make your sung notes staccato. Hold out the sound until the end of the quarter note. Make it full. Make it rich. *Too Baah.* Connect the five to the six: *Meh-room.* Accent on the *Meh.* You can do this. Okay, again." He pressed the keys.

We lifted our scores higher, opened our mouths and sang: *Too Baah. Mee-room.*

He held up his hand. We stopped. "Better," he said. "Don't let your *mi* spread wide. Make it more of a schwa. *Meh.* Again."

Too. Baah. Meh-room.

"Stop. I still heard one spread '*ee.*'" He waved his hand.

We began again. *Too. Baah. Meh-room.*

"Good! Now put some power behind it. What does your score tell you?"

Candice spoke up. "*Fortissimo.*"

"*Fortissimo,*" Dr. A repeated. "Let's have it." He jabbed the keys, counted us in.

Too. Baah. Meh-room.

"Keep going!"

Spar. Gens. So-noom. Per. Say. Puhl-craw. Reh. Gee. Oh-noom.
"Yes, yes, keep going."
Co. Jet. Ohm. Nays. Ahn. Tay. Throw-noom.
Trroh-noom, Dr. A said.
We stopped singing.
"Really roll that *r. Trroh-noom.* Good, that was good. Do it again. But better."

THE FIGHTING OWEN has prepared for explodes around him, then dies down, explodes, then dies down. He has no time to be shocked or scared. He falls into this new life of danger and reprieve easily; a lack of choice makes everything simpler and it helps to know that he is never truly alone. Men surround him and join him in fighting for their homeland. War is not glorious, as the Romantic poets wrote, but he does enjoy the camaraderie. And, it is true, he has not yet reached the front lines. He will get there eventually, he knows, but for now, he and his battalion stay toward the back of the war zone, waiting in trenches. At night, the skies light up with flashes from their artillery.

Every morning, Owen wakes and straps on his steel helmet, a buff jerkin of leather, gauntlets, and rubber waders that go up to his hips. He cannot imagine trench life without the waders. Only yesterday he slogged through two feet of water and mud for two and a half miles in a trench. But, to his mother, on January 10, 1917, he writes: "Have no anxiety. I cannot do a better thing or be in a righter place... W.E.O xxx"

PART OF OWEN'S work included censoring the letters written by the men in his battalion. I think about Owen reviewing these letters written by his fellow soldiers to their loved ones—their mothers, sisters, wives, friends. I wonder what it felt like to cross out their forbidden words, to read about their hopes and fears. Maybe their lists of needed items reminded Owen of the things he wanted his mother to send him. Maybe he recognized himself or his friends in the stories of their days. Maybe he grew weary—

so many of the same hopes and heartbreaks, so many lives that used to be so rich and full and in stark contrast with the fractured lives being led here.

I read in a recent article in *The Telegraph* that over twelve million letters were delivered to soldiers every week during World War I. Each one of the soldier's responses had to be censored. They could not write about their location, the number of troops they were with, or any negative opinions of their superiors. Even a simple mention of the weather could give away information about a troop's whereabouts.

Though Owen mentions the weather often, he rarely gives any detail about his location. Most of my information about where he was posted throughout the war comes from the timeline and from footnotes and headings added by the editors of *Collected Letters*. I flip through the pages of the book. There are 600 pages worth of letters that Owen wrote in his lifetime, most of them from the three years he spent in the military. There are so many letters that I sometimes think I won't finish them all, but then I begin reading, and I forget everything else but Owen and his requests for new socks and his tent full of mud and the voices of his friends echoing from the past as he records their words in letters, and I read them, here in Virginia, one hundred years later.

IN BARCELONA, BENJAMIN meets two men who become some of his closest friends: the composer Lennox Berkeley and the critic and writer Peter Burra. The two men, along with another composer friend, take Britten to a nightclub in Chinatown. It is Britten's first time in a club, and as soon as he walks through the doors, a damp heat wraps around him. Colored lights swirl around him and men with painted eyes and pretty dresses dance to music. When Britten looks around the room, he sees men together, smoking, laughing, kissing, and doing things he has thought of, but not done. He trains his eyes on the dancers, in their sequins and feathers, shining in the light.

On Easter Sunday, 1917, Owen drinks tea in the cellar with his fellow soldiers, a bit of Sunday calm about them. The tea warms his hands, and when Owen closes his eyes, he imagines that the cup he holds is not the one issued by the army, but is instead one of the simple tea cups of his childhood. He pretends that his mother has just filled his cup from their familiar kettle and that if he were to open his eyes, he would see spring flowers blooming in front of their kitchen window.

He opens his eyes and remembers: he is in France. He is a soldier fighting for his country. Even so, he lets his shoulders relax and stretches out his legs as he sits in the cool dark of the cellar. Moments of peace are treasures he had not known to count before war. He sips his tea. He talks and laughs with the other men.

A shattering. Machine guns shoot from above. Owen stands, dropping his tea, and rushes up from the cellar. He looks to the sky. A German airplane leaks deep, ballooning smoke and falls in a doomed arc toward the ground. Owen checks his pocket for his pistol and runs over the fields toward the fallen plane. His feet are blistered and bruised, but he does not feel them.

What draws him to the crash? He moves without thinking. His feet carry him over the familiar, barren landscape: dirt and faded grass, open fields that look as gray as the sky and stretch into nothing. The broken machine rises before him. An Albatross. Dark green and tan with the German black cross on its flank and tail. Owen stops before the smoking plane and then creeps closer.

The pilot slumps over the steering wheel, blood dripping from his helmet. He is motionless. How can it be that only seconds ago this man held a beating heart, blood that flowed for a purpose? Owen crouches beside him and reaches into the man's leather coat. He fumbles for the pocket and finds inside a handkerchief. Owen pulls it out and examines it. It is plain—except for a spatter of blood in one corner. He pockets it for his brother as a souvenir, and takes a step back from the pilot to regard the destroyed plane. Owen walks alongside it. How would it feel to fly? To look down and see the war from above? All of this fighting would appear insignificant. Owen and his fellow soldiers would look like nothing more than clods of dirt. Like the clay from which they began.

As Owen retreats from the plane and makes toward camp, his men scurry out to ask what he found. It still strikes him that he is their officer, their superior. He feels too young for such responsibility. Owen tells them of the dead German, the plane's impressive frame. They return to the hut and Owen notices that his men have picked up his fallen teacup. They soon settle back into the quiet.

Tomorrow, Owen's men will dig out the engines and the guns from the plane, and he will go back to censoring letters. He wonders when he will receive orders to advance to the front lines—it could be at any time, as sudden and surprising as a plane falling from the sky on a Sunday afternoon.

I sit in my kitchen with the slanted floors and I read and reread Owen's letters. His mother saved every single one and bound them in stacks with bits of ribbon and string. Because she kept every letter, and because she was generous enough to give them to her son Harold, who wanted to gather them into a published book, I am able to read more than five hundred letters that Owen wrote over the course of his lifetime. He could never have imagined that almost one hundred years after he died, a young woman from the United States would carry a heavy book of his collected letters in her book bag and read the words he had written to his mother, his sister, his friends.

I turn the pages of *Wilfred Owen: Collected Letters* and stop at the pictures. In one, he poses with the officers of the 5th Reserve Battalion, the Manchester Regiment, in 1916. He sits cross-legged in the front row, and his gloved hands grip a riding crop or cane of sorts. A dimple thumbs the bottom of his chin and a light mustache grazes his lip. His eyes smile and his mouth turns upward almost imperceptibly. He is handsome. More handsome than the other men in his regiment, I observe, with—why?—a feeling of pride.

From the time that I write this, the photo was taken ninety-six years ago. In it, Owen is twenty-three years old. My age. I feel as if I know him—like a distant cousin, maybe. I have read the letters he wrote as a child, seen the drawings he scribbled in the margins: horses at first, then, when he was older, when he was preparing to leave military training and go to battle, broken legs and men with bullets in their heads.

Maybe I think of Owen as a cousin because I have a cousin who went to war. Hans went to Iraq as part of Operation Iraqi Freedom when I was in high school. He drove Humvees. Passed out candy to children on the streets. His sister, Annika, wrote a letter to him every day. I wrote few because I never knew what to say to him. Would my normal, everyday life make him sad?

When I was younger, I had a crush on Hans. He had blond hair, blue eyes, and an amazing voice he used to serenade our grandmother at holidays. I remember picking him up at the Greyhound station with my mother and brother, once, when I was around ten. He had been visiting his father, a Vietnam veteran, in Maine and took the bus back to Minnesota. We picked him up in Minneapolis and dragged him along on our errands before bringing him back to his mother's house in the rural, southern part of the state. My mother bought a pair of eyeglasses while my little brother, Hans, and I sat on a bench outside. Teenage girls, closer to Hans's age than my own, walked past us, and Hans kept saying, "There's a cute chick." To my younger brother, "Max, do you see that chick?"

Max was little and thought he meant a baby chicken. He kept getting up and looking beneath the bench. "Where? Where?" he asked.

"Do you know who the biggest chick is, though? Your sister." Hans smiled at me.

When a rocket-propelled grenade hit Hans's Humvee, shrapnel flew into his face and eye. His head, locked in its helmet, hit the hard metal of the Humvee. As a combat-wounded veteran, Hans was awarded three Purple Hearts. Though the physical injuries were horrific, nothing compares to the pain of survivor's guilt, the vivid flashbacks, and the myriad symptoms of Post-Traumatic Stress Disorder that he has experienced over the course of the last many years. Even now, almost fifteen years later, Hans cannot fully escape the war.

BULLETS SCREAM PAST Owen's head and he dives into the dirt. Sprays of shells hit the ground in waves and Owen hears shouts and booms and thick *pock* sounds. Sounds of flesh and bullets colliding. He gets up, crouches low to the ground, and presses on. He yanks his helmet strap and cinches it tighter. Shells rain down around him, and still Owen runs toward the German trenches up ahead until he watches the enemies slide and disappear into their trenches. Relief washes over him. There will be no need to use his bayonet.

Owen and his men stay on the Line for the next twelve days. They do not wash their faces. They do not take off their boots. They barely sleep. At night, the men lie in holes and wake at the slightest sound—a shell could come and blast them all at any moment.

And it does. A shell hits the top of a nearby bank and Owen, still asleep in a trench, launches into the air. He wakes while flying through sprays of dirt and rock and he yells out. He lands and opens his eyes to see a friend, in pieces, strewn about him. Owen lies in his friend's blood, feels it seep through his uniform, feels it grow cold. He cannot move, he can only shake and squeeze his eyes shut. Wait.

IN 1934, BRITTEN'S father dies. Britten cannot work. He extends deadlines for his incomplete suite and then extends them again. When his family celebrates Christmas together in Lowestoft, they sit about, listless, with feigned cheer in their smiles. The fire cracks and sputters behind the grate while air shakes the window panes. Outside, down the road, the sea churns and crashes into itself over and over. What would it be like to sink down to the ocean floor? Britten imagines how dark, how quiet it must be. Is that what death is? He cannot imagine true and lasting silence. Everything in him is heavy. His composing feels far away, unattainable. He cannot find enough space inside of himself for new notes and melodies. The same line, long and mournful, plays itself over and over in his mind and he cannot break its loop. His father is dead, the melody says, he is dead and in the end, compositions can change nothing about life and death. He looks out the window and tries to look over and past the sea toward something—anything—else.

In 2014, I leave my house in Virginia and go home to Minnesota for Christmas. I sit at the kitchen table in the home where I grew up and look out the windows at the backyard. I pick at my hangnails and watch the snow fall lazily, fat flakes arcing in wide circles on their way to the ground. I try to imagine snow like this falling on the empty land where Owen waited and charged ahead and then waited some more. Would anyone have found falling snow like this pretty then? Probably not. The monotony of the cold and snow and frozen ground must have made time stop.

I watch a deer walk down by the creek, stripping small twigs and branches of their bark. Before long, two more deer enter my field of vision, then another, and another. My father keeps the bird feeders full of suet and sunflower seeds, and squirrels wobble their way across the wires and up the plastic cones. Naked trees scrape the sky and bushes lean together as though for warmth.

The majority of his time at war, Owen lived and fought on a wide space of land that had once held much wildlife. Rabbits and songbirds would have flitted about in tall grasses and wildflowers. Trees would have grown heavy with thick, green leaves. Explosions, gunshots, and the impact of shells shook the earth and felled trees. The land burned to a blank char. The empty expanse that spread before Owen would have reminded him again and again of things missing—of life missing.

I sit in a warm kitchen, but I always complain that it's too cold in here. I watch individual snowflakes fall to the ground. When a flake blends in with the white, I flick my eyes up to the skies again and pick a new one. I do not know what it is to have danger at my back.

Wilfred Owen: a hundred years ago, you were sleeping in snow.

You are not forgotten.

I cannot stop thinking about you.

Owen and the rest of his company walk toward a freezing winter, a deep white unknown. Owen hunches over with his head down. Snow flecks his dark hair, pricks his cheeks. Worse than the dugouts and the mud and the water is the snow. Bullets fly through the white expanse around them and they lie on their bellies, grow wet, smell the sour scent of their sopping wool uniforms. He can see nothing for miles, just white, just snow. Every so often a dark shadow circling, a hawk.

Owen sets his jaw each morning as part of his uniform. Everywhere he looks, ugliness. Even the words that spill from his own mouth—ugly. He cannot stop shaking. He screams in the night. Visions visit him: his friend's arm centimeters away from his hand, a leg nowhere to be seen.

In a postscript to his mother on February 4, 1917:

> I suppose I can endure cold, and fatigue, and the face-to-face death, as well as another; but extra for me there is the universal pervasion of Ugliness. Hideous landscapes, vile noises…everything unnatural, broken, blasted; the distortion of the dead, whose unburiable bodies sit outside the dug-outs all day, all night, the most execrable sights on earth. In poetry we call them the most glorious. But to sit with them all day, all night…
>
> I have to write it down for the sake of future reminders…of how incomparable is an innocent and quiet life…
>
> Again, dearest love to all. W.E.O.

I READ THAT in June of 1917, Owen gets sent to Craiglockhart Hospital, just outside Edinburgh, Scotland, after shaking and suffering nightmares for weeks in various hospitals and clearing stations. I want to know what Craiglockhart looks like. I search online and find photographs of a large brick building with high windows, multiple floors, and lush lawns that roll out from the hospital on all sides. I see both black-and-white photos from around the time that Owen would have been there, and more recent photos in full color. The building still stands.

After World War I, the hospital was sold to the Society of the Sacred Heart and became a convent, then a school for training Roman Catholic teachers. Today, the building houses the Edinburgh Napier University's Business School. It also holds the University's War Poets Collection, which contains documents, films, and photographs about the soldiers who stayed there. Prominently displayed are works by Wilfred Owen and his dear friend and fellow soldier-poet and Craiglockhart patient, Siegfried Sassoon.

Dr. W.H.R. Rivers and Dr. Arthur Brock treated Owen and Sassoon, whom Owen met at the hospital. Both doctors are credited with revolutionizing treatment for neurasthenia, more commonly known during World War I as shell shock, or what is known today as Post-Traumatic Stress Disorder. Dr. Rivers developed the "talking cure," which encouraged soldiers to talk about their experiences in war. This directly challenged the strong façade that soldiers felt they needed to keep up despite the suffering they'd endured. Dr. Brock thought that shell shock patients should keep busy instead of sitting in silence with their thoughts and traumatic memories. He encouraged Owen to write through his horror and fear. Owen and Sassoon are not the only ones who received groundbreaking mental care during World War I—in the Craiglockhart hospital alone, the small staff of doctors and nurses treated between 1,500 and 1,800 soldiers who suffered from shell shock.

SIEGFRIED SASSOON HAS an open, upward looking face, like a cloud backlit by sun. The two poets admire one another and become fast friends, talking about what they have seen and felt, but always in terms of verse, meter, rhyme. Sassoon teaches Owen the value of vernacular, the effect of irony. Slowly, his influence helps Owen pare down the flourishes and Romantic characteristics that he absorbed from Keats and Shelley.

Later in his life, Sassoon wrote of Owen: "I discovered that Wilfred had endured worse things than I had realized from the little he told me... His thick dark hair was already touched with white above the ears. As I remember him during those months we spent together at Craiglockhart he was consistently cheerful."

Nobody knew.

Nobody knew the terror that filled him, slick and dark like oil, the minute he closed his eyes. Nobody knew the way the earth pulled out from under him again and again. How the shell erupted and he went flying. Over and over he was thrown across the earth. Over and over he landed in front of his friend, face to face with death.

DR. A HAD explained to us when the tenor and baritone soloists would sing, but their parts weren't included in our choral scores. We were learning the *War Requiem* in messy, jagged chunks. I had no idea how everything was supposed to sound all together and, for the first time, I started dreading choir. Dr. A charged forward, however, and we had no choice but to follow him, to trust him when he said that we could do this.

"Today we're going to work on another section of the *Dies Irae*." Dr. A opened his giant score. He held it up to us. "Page forty-three. Let's go. Sopranos, start us off. Rehearsal number thirty. Measure 180. *Quid sum miser tunc dicturus. What shall I, a wretch, say then?*"

Whoever had the score before me had scribbled circles around half the notes on my page and had drawn little arrows above some of them. I took her markings to mean that some of the notes needed to be sung higher than sounded right. All of the circles next to the accidentals told me that it would be easy to go flat or sharp in this section.

Dr. A gave us a D on the piano. "Sing on *ta*," he said. "We'll throw in the Latin later."

We began. The first two notes were D's, then an E flat, all eighth notes, easy enough. Then another eighth note back on the D. I tried to look one note ahead of what I sang. Then an E natural. An E natural was a half-step higher than an E flat, naturally, but what did that sound like? Wait—what key were we in? Who was I kidding—how would knowing that help me? The E natural connected to two notes on ascending half steps. Thank God these were all eighth notes. F#. G#. Where did those come from? I stopped singing. I opened and closed my mouth a few times and tried to look as though I was still singing, but then I stopped that, too, and just stared at the page. I listened to the sopranos around me. The majority sang on the same note, but a few outliers *Ta-ta*'ed a little above and below everyone else. I didn't want to guess where I had been singing.

Dr. A held up his hand. "Let's try again," he said.

We had just begun, and already I needed to take off my sweater and scarf. My stomach grumbled and I put a hand on it, tried to muffle the sound. I hadn't eaten much for lunch, and I hadn't had time for my usual granola bar between class and choir. Dr. A gave us a fresh D, and we started again. The sharps and naturals traded places in such quick succession that the notes sounded squashed on top of each other, scrambled in a crazed mass of notes and rests, singing and quick breathing. I couldn't find my way inside of the music.

When I tried to sing my *ta-ta-ta*s, I imagined fingers rubbing together and in between the thumb and forefinger all the notes I tried to sing were being tamped down and jumbled up. Dr. A told us to stop again and played the two measures four times in a row. I listened and tried to envision the notes flowing into me and staying there. We tried again, but the notes refused to stick. I looked at the page, at the Latin words cramped together. The notes slithered across the staff like a snake. The section was short, and yet I couldn't keep up. The score shook in my hands. The pages faded away from me. My cheeks went from hot to cold. I blinked at my score and watched it turn white. I realized that I couldn't hear Candice or Liz on either side of me.

I sat down with my elbows on my knees and put my head on my score. Candice whispered something to me, her long brown hair brushing my arms as she bent toward me. I lifted a hand to say I was okay. I breathed, and slowly I could hear the notes crawling up their strange scales again.

I felt a hand on my arm. Candice sat down next to me. "You okay?"

Liz reached down and rubbed my back. I took a few deep breaths, found my place in the score, and stood back up.

After we finished rehearsal, Candice and I put our scores back in their slots and walked toward the campus café. We talked about how difficult it was to learn the *War Requiem* and we wondered why Dr. A had chosen this piece of music. It would certainly make us grow as musicians if we ever succeeded in reading the notes correctly, but the music wasn't anything like what we usually sang for our spring concert. It wasn't pretty. It was harsh, strained, and ugly.

FRUSTRATION AND DESPAIR quake beneath the surface of Britten's skin. His father is dead, he writes music in halting spurts, and in 1937, Britten's friend Peter Burra dies in a light aircraft accident. Shocked and grieving, Burra's friends gather to give a toast to their friend and discuss what to do with his writings and personal effects. They decide that his oldest friend, Peter Pears, and his newest friend, Britten, will be the ones to go to his house and sort through his letters and personal effects before others get the chance to look over them.

Shortly after, Britten waits just inside his home for Peter Pears to arrive. It is a warm spring night, the air heavy and damp. He sees the single headlamp shining out from a motorbike, the road and surrounding trees displayed in a momentary tunnel of light. Pears pulls up before the house and cuts the engine. Britten watches him run a hand through his hair, notes his high brow and strong nose illumined by moonlight. Pears looks up at the door and Britten steps out to meet him in the night.

Pears's hand is large and warm and doesn't grip Britten's pianist's hand too tight. Britten climbs onto the back of Pears's motorbike and slides his arms around his waist. He feels solid, safe. Pears turns on the ignition, frees the clutch plates, and kick-starts the bike. It gives a roar and then settles into a rumble beneath them. With a small jerk, Pears lets up on the clutch and they start toward Burra's house in Berkshire. They haven't been on the road long when the clouds split open and a torrential rain falls down on them. Britten hangs onto Pears when they turn corners and speed along the long stretches of slick road. They arrive at Burra's after midnight, damp and cold and breathing hard in the mist and rain.

Together, Britten and Pears sort through stacks of their friend's writings, side by side on the couch. "Look at this one," Pears says, holding out a sheet of paper to Britten. "I wrote this to Peter years and years ago. I can't believe he kept it." Britten reaches out and drifts his fingers across the words Pears had written. He knows he imagines it, but the page feels warm, alive. Britten can feel the sorrow roll off Pears in waves. He wants to absorb it for him, though he feels overwhelmed by his own loss of their friend. In the midst of all the grief, though, Britten feels a spark of something—warmth? Hope? Interest?—in the man beside him.

STILL IN CRAIGLOCKHART, Owen wakes to gunshots in his dreams. Bullets on flesh. Crunches of bone. Moans of men dying, men almost dead. He does not want to sleep. It is too real. Even if the sounds he hears come from his mind, his damaged mind, the dreams must correlate to some battle happening in real time. Maybe in Germany or Russia or Belgium—someone is killing and someone is dying. Some soldier like him takes his last breath.

Owen writes and writes. Every time a dream shakes him, he remembers what Sassoon told him: "Sweat your guts out writing poetry."

Sometimes his handwriting is a furious scrawl, sometimes it is as light and delicate as English spring rain. He writes and keeps writing. He revises. Scratches out, changes words, pushes himself to write what is true. He knows he will never again be the little boy running outside with Romantic words spinning through his head. War has killed something inside of him. He writes and knows he works for something bigger than himself, bigger than this war. He is writing for all wars, for all men who died for nothing.

LATER THAT YEAR, in 1937, Britten's mother dies of a heart attack. For weeks, gray rain everywhere he looks. But still—the stirrings of music pulse inside of him, beat against his loneliness. Britten completes another composition, an ode in music to his dear teacher, Frank Bridge. The piece, "Variations on a Theme of Frank Bridge" is performed in Salzburg as the centerpiece of English string music. Though Britten could not attend due to another performance engagement, Peter Pears could and did.

A few days after the performance, Britten holds a letter from Pears in his hands. He studies the handwriting, already growing familiar to him. He reads: "Well, Benjie…I have dashed to the hotel so that I can write down at once something about the concert." He then writes about the music—its delivery, the conducting. Pears is also a capable musician: a vocalist, a tenor, a man who works as hard on his craft as Britten himself does.

I OPEN THE door to my small balcony in Virginia and walk outside. The days are shorter than when I left for the holidays, the air colder. The waxy leaves on the tree next to me look indigo against the pale blue dusk. I can hear my Decca recording of the *War Requiem* from inside. The baritone and tenor soloists' voices are so familiar, they might be neighbors conversing across the way. I don't stay outside for long. If there is no sunset—if only grayish blue clouds cover the sky like they do right now—I hate the moment when the world first goes dark. I feel alone. Lonely.

I go inside and shut the door against the night. I light candles. I sit down at my kitchen table. On the wall above it, I have taped black and white photographs of Benjamin Britten and Wilfred Owen alongside maps of Europe and important dates and poems on Post-its. A movement finishes and I turn off the music. I put my hands to the laptop keys, but they do not move, not at first. I read the Latin Mass for the Dead, which is on the wall just to the right of where I sit. I sway to music I hear in my head. I hear it all: the strings, the brass, the woodwinds, the timpani and snare, the tenor and alto harmony lines, the voices of my friends Candice and Liz on either side of me. I will never forget this music. I will carry it as I do the "Our Father" in French, which I learned in the eighth grade, or the *West Side Story* choreography I danced in high school, or the drum beat my grandfather taught me to tap out with the tips of my fingernails. *Ba-dum-ba-dum-ba-dum. Ba-dum-ba-dum-ba-dum. Ba-dum-ba-dum-ba-dum-ba-dum-ba-dum-DA! ba-da-dum.*

WAR HANGS JUST above Europe. For the past many months, Britten and Pears have watched their friends and fellow artists cloak themselves in worry. In the face of the unknown, they make music together, Britten on the piano and Pears singing, his rich tenor warming each song note by note. Britten feels as though he could forget all else in the world as long as he listened to Pears's voice.

But the world intervenes. The threat of war pulses beyond—but just beyond—them. If war did erupt in Europe, Britten is sure that he would not be able to fight or kill, not when the whole of his life is devoted to creation. And perhaps leaving could provide other opportunities; his teacher Frank Bridge had enjoyed great success in America, his friend Wystan Auden had left for America three months prior, and Britten could organize an American tour.

He poses the question to Pears one evening. The wine is poured, the ginger cookies on a plate. On the piano, a score sits open; their primary mode of communication is through music. But now they speak, not sing, and they let the possibilities—of America, of all that could happen in America—stretch between them, a fermata over a whole rest. They look at each other, questions in their eyes, nervous hands occupied by wine glasses. Yes, they decide, they will go. They will see to whatever awaits them, hoping they can return to quiet evenings spent singing and playing, eating cookies and talking about music.

OWEN CLOSES HIS eyes while in bed in Craiglockhart. He sees them, bent and crumpled into the mud, their skin gray and green and rotting in the damp earth. Crusted blood streaks from holes in their coats. Their boots are gone, scavenged. Blackened, bloated feet remain. The toenails, often toes themselves, have fallen off. How did men walk on feet so puffed and soft they look like putty? Sometimes the feet are so black that they shine in the light as if they'd been dipped in oil. Sometimes greenish bubbles rise from the flesh. Were these feet really ones that had been kissed by mothers when young? Had these feet that had once run across beaches and fields in happy sunlight?

Now dead.

Bodies. Always more bodies. Bodies from England, France, and Russia. From India, West Africa, and America. From Germany and Austria-Hungary and so many more. So many dead. With his eyes closed, Owen tries to see the fields the way they must have been, once. He can't. He can only see the trees cracked and burned and mostly gone. The land pockmarked by shells. The bodies. Always, always, the bodies.

BRITTEN AND PEARS stay with acquaintances William and Elizabeth Mayer in Amityville, New York, in 1939. A month passes, two. War begins to rumble through Europe like thunder signaling a disastrous storm. Germany has invaded Poland, and after the German U-boat, U-30, invades and sinks the British passenger ship, the SS *Athenia*, Britain declares war on Germany. France, Australia, New Zealand, Canada, and South Africa follow.

Britten and Pears stay in Amityville in between concert dates on their separate tours of America. The Mayers are kind people, German refugees who fled from Nazi persecution in 1936. Mr. Mayer is a doctor and Mrs. Mayer a proud and supportive patron of the arts. She loves keeping her home bursting with artists. Many weekends, Wystan Auden sits in the dining room writing poems and puffing cigarettes. Britten sketches symphonies, writes letters to his sisters, and scores an opera about Paul Bunyan for which Auden writes the book.

Britten and Pears trade off time in the house for their working hours. Pears goes for walks while Britten works and Britten occupies himself while Pears sings, sometimes stopping mid-sentence in a book to listen to him practice. Pears has been taking lessons in New York City and his voice sounds more supported than ever before. Listening to him, Britten can sometimes hear snippets of melodies that he wants to write for Pears's voice, for his rounded, floating sound. Sometimes, Pears will take a breath and look at him, and Britten knows that he remembers, too: that night in Grand Rapids shortly after they arrived in America. That night when they held each other and knew.

EVEN THOUGH NIGHT has already fallen in Virginia, I pack my laptop, journal, and books of letters into my backpack and drive to the library. I spread out my books on a large table and plug my headphones into my laptop so that I can listen to the *Requiem* as I work. I begin writing, but before long, I stop. I sit at the table with my hands in my lap, and I listen to the music with more focus and intention than I feel while driving, or reading, or talking on the phone with a friend. I have listened to these movements so many times that I can hear, now, mistakes made by the choir. I know when they are a quarter-beat late to their entrance, and when the sopranos have not taken a breath deep enough to support the high arc of the fugue in the sixth movement.

I open my internet browser and go to the website of the *War Requiem*'s publisher, Boosey and Hawkes. I search for the *Requiem*'s page and find information about the composition. Beneath the title, I find a repertoire note that says "Choral level of difficulty: Level 5 (5 greatest)." I shake my head and laugh. Of course the *War Requiem* is one of the most difficult choral pieces to sing. Didn't I know that already? Hadn't I learned that firsthand when I trudged into rehearsal every Monday, Wednesday, and Friday of Chapel Choir? I wonder what would have happened if Dr. A had told us how difficult the piece would be. How much can we accomplish when we head toward the unknown but believe, somehow, that we will reach the places we need to go?

OWEN ISN'T THE only one who wakes yelling and kicking in the night. They all do. The men they killed visit them in the darkness. The dead men clutch guts that spill from their bayonet wounds. Blood falls from their mouths in gurgling currents. Others drag themselves, legless, across the floor, leaving trails of blood and dirt. These are the killed, and the living are the killers. Punished. That is what's happening to them. They are being punished. The soldiers wake themselves screaming. In that moment when they open their eyes and the dead men vanish, they know, with a clarity so cool and sharp it stings, that they are still in hell, even though they sleep between clean sheets at Craiglockhart.

IN 1939, BRITTEN spends two weeks in Chicago's wet and freezing cold while he rehearses his piano concerto with the Illinois Symphony Orchestra. He will play the piano solo himself for his American debut.

On his way to and from rehearsals, Britten takes taxis through the Chicago streets, where snow swirls in angry spirals between skyscrapers.

He watches people hurry across bridges, bundled in scarves and hats. The cold wind coming off the lake reminds him of winter at his family home in Suffolk. Here in Chicago, protected from the wind and snow, he sits back in the cab and sneaks a hand into the breast pocket of his overcoat to touch the letters he keeps there. One from Beth, one from Barbara. These letters have flown across an ocean from his sisters' fingertips to his.

Sometimes, as now, he looks at the strange city outside his window and doesn't know how the world can be so large. How is it that he and these people walking the streets are so far away from his home and the trouble that is slowly creeping up and crushing Europe? The Soviet Union has invaded both Poland and Finland and has taken over Estonia, Lithuania, and Latvia. The United States has declared its neutrality, and Britten can't help but feel that, like America, he is turning his back on the war in order to keep himself safe. Even though he truly does believe in pacifism, guilt plagues him.

Britten keeps a few other slim envelopes from his family of sorts here in America. Mrs. Mayer writes dutifully, wishing him well in his American debut and telling him of the boredom that has come over Amityville since he left. Pears writes, too, of his lessons and trips to New York City. Britten clings to the last lines of his letter where Pears's love is scrawled in his steady and easy hand.

The cab pulls to a stop and Britten hands the driver the bland green bills. He stretches and flicks his fingers in his gloves, hating the way the cold makes his hands go numb. He thinks of the fast fingerings and widespread chords he must play—perfectly—in just a few days. He opens the door and puts his head down against the wind, walking briskly toward rehearsal, trying not to slip.

OWEN KEEPS BUSY at the insistence of Dr. Brock. The men in Craiglockhart do all sorts of things: weave, go on walks, put on plays. Despite the activities and hours spent in therapy, some of the soldiers still shake, some still can't walk, and some can barely speak. Owen is in better shape than most, but he can't rid himself of the dreams. Some of the dreams are new every time he closes his eyes. Others are recurring, as familiar to him as his own face or looping handwriting. The shell blasts, he flies, and hits the earth. His dear friend lies in pieces all around him. The shell blasts again, he flies, and hits the earth. He flies and hits the earth. Hits the earth. Hours and days pass in his dreams.

In the morning, when he sips milk from a glass tumbler, Owen thinks that the moment of death must actually be the moment a person wakes from this terrible, inescapable dream where they are almost as dead as the men they killed.

RAGE SIMMERED BETWEEN the notes in the *Dies Irae*, pushing them apart, smashing them together. Dotted eighth notes, double-dotted eighth notes, rests, and triplets cluttered the pages. Dr. A called to us from over the grand piano: "Ground yourselves in the beat. March, march!" We stomped on the risers, made each other shake. *Dies Irae. Day of Wrath.* The deep breaths that plunged into the bottoms of our lungs could power so many ragged screams. We could make sound tear through our throats. We wanted to. We wanted to yell. We didn't know what all of these Latin words meant, but we could feel their meaning bubbling in our blood. We carved out the backs of our throats, let full and rounded tones carry our breath away. We listened to our sound bounce off the high white walls and echo back to us after we cut off a *forte* note. *Di-es-Ir-ae-ae-ae.* Was that us? Did we just produce that sound?

Dr. A looked at us, eyes ablaze. He nodded just a little bit. Slowly, we stopped marching. We felt each other's power all lined up side by side, pulsing beneath our skin, waiting to burst out.

That was it. All we had to do was channel.

"Again," Dr. A said.

We whipped the pages back. I clenched my fists on either side of my score. For the first time, I felt ready.

BRITTEN HAS TO stop the concerto at the beginning of the performance in order to fix some of the piano keys. He stands, waves his arms a little, and apologizes. The audience laughs with him. They are charmed. The piano is fixed and they begin again. Britten plays flawlessly and the orchestra performs much better than he expected.

The next day, he reads the American papers where they say wonderful things about his music. About him, the reviews state that he is "gangling," "loose-jointed," "as English as rain," and even, "a kick-in-the-pants of a young Englishman." Oh, these Americans. He smiles to himself over the newspaper. He opens up the curtains of his hotel room and looks down at the grids of cars below. What a strange place. What strange people. And yet—he wonders if playing at home would mean more, would do more good. He cannot feel at peace knowing all that waits at home.

OWEN WALKS THE grounds surrounding Craiglockhart. He is not allowed far, but it doesn't matter. He can see grass and trees. Life. He crouches down and looks at weeds that grow amidst gravel and bright wildflowers that sway among tall grasses just off the path. He touches the leaves and slim stems, remembering childhood days when he ran along trails near his home, grabbing fistfuls of flowers and weeds. He would gather bunches for his mother, release the bouquets to her and find his palms sticky with bitter sap. He does not pick the flowers now. Instead, he watches their ruffled heads bob up and down in the breeze. It is amazing that these plants can angle themselves toward the sun and feed off its light—plentiful, warm, and clear.

Dr. Brock has suggested that Owen join the Field Club, a group of patients who get together every so often and give each other lectures about nature. He decides he will write his speech about plants and title it "Do Plants Think?" Owen stands and looks to the sun himself. He spreads his fingers in the light and closes his eyes. His eyelids flare orange and he sees iridescent green stripes floating across his closed eyes. He breathes in the fresh scent of grass and, in a small moment of grace, he does not think of the dead men. Before they rush into his thoughts again, he focuses on the warmth of the sun on his palms and face. He doesn't think. He only feels. He is a glowing body standing in the simple, steadfast sun.

THE THINGS BRITTEN hears about the war can't be true—the bombs, the camps, the suffering. Who is he to be saved? A musician, an artist, neither a doctor nor a prime minister. The creeping despair that sometimes overtakes him comes more and more frequently. He develops rashes and suffers nosebleeds and headaches. He cannot sleep. His mind races with ideas, but the minute he sits down to work, everything vanishes into a heavy mist that settles down deep and thick around his mind.

At breakfast one morning, Britten watches Mrs. Mayer pour their coffee with steady hands. She was born in Germany and lived in Munich as a child. How does she feel when she thinks of the terrible role her homeland plays in this war?

Britten imagines Mrs. Mayer as a young girl, a little Elizabeth, running through the cobblestone streets of Munich. She has talked about it before with him, about the beautiful, ornately-carved stone churches, the parks with rose gardens and fountains, the shops painted in rich burgundies and pale greens. It must have been beautiful. And now—so much ugliness seeping out from within.

Does she feel guilty on behalf of her fellow Germans, Britten wonders? No, she hasn't lived there for many years. She finds her home in Amityville now.

What does it mean, what does it really mean to belong to a country? He is English, yes, and he is fiercely proud of his home, but would he die for his country?

He feels almost sure he wouldn't.

Even so, he and Pears write to the British Embassy often and ask if they can come back; it is their home. The response is always negative. It's better to stay there, the Embassy writes, and continue on as artistic ambassadors of sorts. Britten feels far away from England and the rest of the world. He might as well be up in the stars.

WHEN OWEN WRITES home to his mother from Craiglockhart he leaves most things out. The spaces between letters and words holds so much that cannot be said.

Instead, he turns to Sassoon. They read each other's poetry over weak tea and toast. Owen watches Sassoon work over his lines, underlining, crossing out, making notes in the margins. Sassoon looks up, grabs his teacup with his pen still in hand and takes a sip. "You don't need so much," he says. Sassoon shows Owen how to pare down the words, make the meaning punch through them, and Owen nods. They sit in silence, the words still rolling inside them.

Owen rattles the bottom of his cup against the table. He and Sassoon look at each other. A moment passes, in it the question.

"I can't go back," Sassoon says, and downs the last of his tea, "but if we do, we keep writing. We write until we can't anymore."

They turn back to their drafts. When Owen writes his hands feel like his own. They write, they make things. They are not killing—stabbing flesh or squeezing triggers—as they do in his dreams. His mind searches for language to describe how ugly war is. Every time he writes down words that reveal war's truth, a trembling thought bursts inside of him: maybe what he writes can save another. What he writes is just ink on paper, but it is more than that. When he dies, these poems will still be in the world.

I IMAGINE OWEN and Sassoon leaning over their poems together. The lamplight casts long shadows and they alternate between quiet moments of awe and vibrant conversations about various poetic techniques and choices. I picture them passing a pencil back and forth, sharing discoveries and theories on art. I love to envision Owen having a friend—such a kind and understanding friend—who understood every emotion, every question, every dream.

MORE INVASIONS, MORE bombs, more deaths across the ocean. Britten doesn't like America. He doesn't want to be here any longer. This country is too young, too haughty, too rich. He wants to go home, but knows he can't. He must write his music and he can do that most easily here, at the Mayers's. He draws the curtains and sits near the piano. He sketches and writes and blocks out the outside world. It is all he can do. There is no way he could be off fighting in a war. His gifts lie in creation, not destruction. Still, a nagging guilt. Men and women are dying. He looks at the stems of his quarter notes, marching sternly across the page. It is not enough.

OWEN WRITES BECAUSE he has to. Writing is the only way to stave off the dreams. He faces them, he records them in ink, he roots them to the page, and in doing so, he shakes the fear a little more from his mind. That fear, that horror—it will never be gone. He knows this. But at least when he writes he feels he is alive. He remembers that he is not one of the corpses strewn across the barren land, their dead bodies punctured by the dead stumps of trees splayed on the dead, frozen ground. His fingers clamp down around his pencil. His other hand holds down the sheet of paper. Muscles, blood, and nerves make them move. His body is warm. His hand floats across the paper and he spells death with the ink.

Here, in his poetry, he is honest. So few soldiers are. He writes his letters home like everybody else, and, like everybody else, he masks what's in his mind. He smooths the tremors that course through him at night. He blots out the screaming, the terrors, the tears with certain black ink: All is well.

A lie. Even on the days he feels better, a lie. A lie until he dies, he knows.

But then again, guilt whittles at his nerves. He is much better off than so many of his fellow men. They have lost legs and arms and eyes, and, finally, heart. Yells and screams are ripped from their throats each night by demons only they can see. Demons that were personally shaped for them. Demons with faces of the men they killed.

The war has ruined them.

How MUCH CAN be contained in a single phrase? *Dona eis requiem.* Anything and everything. Grant them rest. The notes whispered out of me, got lost in the mesh of voices. I stood next to Candice in rehearsal. We practiced and knew the notes better now. I kept my pencil tucked in my right hand and the score resting lightly on my left palm. I was starting to know when the page turns came and I swayed my head with the rehearsal piano. I stared at Dr. A as he conducted, but I didn't see him anymore. I saw the faces of soldiers marching into battle, never coming back. *Christe Eleison. Christ have mercy upon them.*

OWEN FEELS HIMSELF getting stronger. He writes, he writes, he writes. At night, his dreams are of car crashes, bridges tumbling into dark water—accidents that could happen at any time to anyone, war or no war. He knows he should be happy that his mind is mending and he is, he is. But he knows what awaits him when his papers get stamped, when he buttons up his uniform and straps on his boots.

One morning, Dr. Brock comes in to speak with Owen shortly after he wakes up. "I think you are well enough," he says. His hands hang limp at his sides. "I have sent word."

3. OFFERTORIUM

"Tibi Domine laudis offerimus."

"We offer to thee sacrifices and prayers."

How CAN HE possibly go back? Owen has received his orders: he will be shipped away from Craiglockhart tomorrow morning and the world will be ripped out from under him once again. Jolts of metallic adrenaline rush through his chest at the thought of any boom or crack. He is now more afraid than ever of being sent back to battle because he has seen everything there is to see except his own death. He understands why Sassoon said he couldn't go back. Owen has heard that he will be stationed at a hotel in Scarborough on the North Sea, about two hundred miles south of Craiglockhart, but who knows how long he will be there? The year is 1917. The United States has just passed an act that will allow its government to draft young men for the war instead of depending on volunteers. From what Owen can see, there will be no end.

For the past few months, Owen has been working hard for his body and mind to heal, but now—now that he is less broken, he will be sent back to be shattered again.

Anger beats at the inside of his chest. He is angry at his doctor for believing that he should be sent back. Angry at Germany and at all the countries involved in this war. Angry at the old men who sit debating battle plans at desks while young soldiers follow orders and lose their lives. And he is angry at himself for enlisting in the first place. Why did he do it? Did he really think that he could help England win the war? He is one man, and he now knows more than ever that he is a poet, not a fighter.

Owen looks around the sitting room at the soldiers. Some sit alone, others with one or two companions. They play cards, they read, they stare into space, and they shake, their newspapers quaking between their fingertips. When Owen sees these men, he cannot help but see the boys they must have been just a few years ago, running and shouting in wide fields beside their homes. If they hadn't fought in this war, they would have been falling in love, working steady jobs, and coming home to their families every evening. Their days would have been full of promise and warmth. Instead, they are here, screaming in pain, or they are in trenches with rotting feet and graying hair, or they are dead.

He must keep writing. He must work to tear down that false promise of war's glory that turns boys into dead men, whether they die in battle or come out alive.

I READ IN a biography written by his brother that Wilfred Owen had premonitions of an early death beginning as a teenager. I wonder if he sensed that he would die within the year after being released from Craiglockhart. At the time I write this, I am approaching the age Owen was when he died, and I am beginning to understand now how young that is. This morning I woke up to bird chatter and took my mug of coffee on a walk around the neighborhood. I watched cloud shadow and light play across quiet mountains and I thought about words that I might write down when I returned home. I breathed in air and sun and bird song. Twenty-five years on this earth is barely any time at all.

RAIN BEATS DOWN on the window panes and huge booms of thunder shake the old Amityville house. Lightning illuminates the room, and for brief flashes Britten can see everything as if it were daytime. The bureau piled with Pears's unfolded sweaters, the stacks of books and papers on the chair in the corner, the solid mountain of Pears's shoulder rising beside him.

When the house shakes, the corner joists rattle and remind Britten of the sound of tightening strings. Once, as a child, he wound the E string on his viola too tight. Clicks echoed from the instrument, like a train going over tracks in a cavernous tunnel. Before it snapped, he loosened it while exhaling, remembering his mother's warning that a snapping string could take out an eye.

Now, with the house shaking beneath claps of thunder, Britten thinks of his sisters and their families, and of his dear friends, all back in England. Raids and bombs must sound something like this. What would it really sound like for a house to crumble, to collapse? The thunder comes in shorter intervals now. The storm must be just above him. Britten lies on his back and tries to stare past the ceiling, past the roiling black clouds, to an expanse of starry sky that is quiet and calm.

Thunder again. He jolts back to himself. What is he doing here? Here, in America? Overseas, his people fight. Overseas, his people die. And here he is in a comfortable home near a tranquil bay, an ocean away from the war.

What does it matter, his music? What does music matter when people are dead?

Icy hands seem to clutch his chest. He cannot breathe. He reaches for Pears, who, somehow, despite the storm, still sleeps. Without opening his eyes or stirring much, Pears drapes an arm around Britten's chest and pulls him close. Britten lets himself be held. He breathes.

WHEN WE WERE a month out from our performance, Dr. A extended our rehearsals by a half hour each day and we started practicing with the orchestra. I loved singing with the orchestra during past performances, and I was excited to see how they would complement our singing this time. It took the choir about five measures of listening to the orchestra play the first movement to realize that if the *War Requiem* were a peanut butter and jelly sandwich, the choir was only the thin coat of jelly. When it had only been us in rehearsal, it was easy to believe that we were the featured artists; our scores showed only the choral parts. Now, we knew that we were integral, yes, but we were not the substance. I felt confused. This was supposed to be our concert, the Chapel Choir concert.

Why wouldn't we sing something that featured us a bit more? Why would Dr. A choose this piece, of all those we might have sung?

The strings dragged their bows across their instruments and I felt a twinge in my chest. They played beautifully. The chimes rang out and Dr. A gave us our entrance. Quiet, worried, we sang into a web of drawn-out, almost stagnant notes. The orchestra created a new space in the music for us to enter. We weren't just singing to a wall anymore—we were singing into a relationship with a hundred other people.

The orchestra was skilled. They showed up to rehearsal confident in their entrances, their runs, the best times to turn the page. I often felt intimidated by the players. They knew their instruments so well. The bows seemed to grow from the string players' fingers like extra limbs. The even breath used to sustain long notes of the bassoon and flute and clarinet must have been something the musicians practiced every day while showering, walking to and from class, standing in line for coffee.

When Dr. A held up his hands and made us stop after a mistake, it was almost always because of the choir. The orchestra kept time like a metronome. Sometimes we fell behind. We couldn't always discern our entrances with so much music going on around us. Whenever I lost my place, I remembered a trick I had heard in grade school about how movie extras mouthed the word "watermelon" over and over to feign true speech. "Watermelon, watermelon," I fake sang and peeked at Candice's score. I could always depend on her for page numbers because she never lost her place.

IN THE SUMMER of 1917, Owen receives instructions to move to Scarborough for the Camp Commandant position of the Hotel Northern Cavalry Barracks at the Clifton Hotel. He keeps the hotel running smoothly, ordering groceries, finding rooms for guests, taking stock of the wine and tobacco stores, and keeping all of the orderlies, kitcheners, and cooks in order. He wakes with the sun to see that breakfast is set at the proper time, and his day continues from there. The work never ceases.

Owen thinks of his poetry in quick flashes throughout the day, but there is not much time to sit and think, to dream and tie down those dreams with ink. At Craiglockhart, Owen spent hours by himself writing and revising. Even in the trenches, even as his feet rotted in the muck, he found his mind floating to verses and stresses and rhythms and rhymes. He had to—there had been no other way to survive.

One night, Owen shines his shoes more vigorously than usual and heads to the Mess Dance. The night is brisk and Owen buttons his coat against the cold wind. He listens to the sound of his shoes crunching on the pavement, and he remembers the summer he spent in Bordeaux walking the beautiful grounds, smelling the wildflowers, tilting his face toward the sun. Owen smiles to think of the dragonflies alighting on the swaying birch and poplar branches. Everything was simple then. He'd adored the Romantics. He'd written about love and nature and felicity.

How could he have known then all that would happen in such a short span of time? He'd left the conversation of the Romantics as soon as he entered into war's clutch. Glory and Romanticism did not belong in this world of war, in this life, his life. Everything had changed.

He was now one voice—though a voice slowly gaining strength—in a new conversation with poetry and its purpose. Poetry still had power over him, but it was a different poetry now.

A poetry that told the truth.

Owen sees the hall in the distance. Yellow light from inside illuminates the windows. He can see shadows of men leaning over the balcony banisters while they look out to sea, the fireflies of their cigarettes swirling orange against the darkness. He picks up his pace, eager to see the old Witley non-commissioned officers that he has heard will be there. He has not seen them since before his hospitalization. Owen marches up the steps to the hall and opens the door.

Groups of men stand with paper cups of punch in their hands. Owen approaches the group nearest him; he recognizes a few of the officers. When they turn to him, their faces pale and their eyes widen in disbelief. "We thought you were dead," they say, quietly at first, and then louder. Other groups look over to him and Owen hears them shout across the hall: "Owen's alive!" More men come over and shake his hand

and say "Welcome back," as though he really had been dead, as though the shell that launched him through the air had killed him instead of just killing something inside him. Owen smiles, but he can feel his eyes freeze in a dark stare. He had been dead to these men.

He remembers the dreams he had had growing up: his face, ghostly and bloated, in a pool of black water. He shudders and one of the men beside him shouts for the hall door to be closed.

Owen tries to smile more brightly. He is not dead. He is not the man in the dream. Owen heard he is marked for Permanent Home Service. He hopes this is true. He will believe it because he has to believe it. When a friend hands him a paper cup, Owen accepts the punch with open hands.

WHAT MUST IT have been like to know that after four years, he was going home? Finally, in 1942, after many letters and pleas, England allowed Britten and Pears to return home. I imagine Britten standing on the ship's deck with Pears. Their hands overlap on the cold, damp rail. The sea sprays their faces and overcoats with a fine mist. They rock toward England, a broken place, their home.

I wonder if they felt as though they had abandoned England. Somehow, I believe that Britten would have plagued himself with more guilt than Pears. I like to imagine Pears wrapping an arm around Britten and telling him that everything was as it should be, that his music was meant to be his contribution to the world, not the pointless giving of his life, because—*Let's face it, Benjie,* I imagine him saying, *You skinny little thing, you would have never lasted more than five minutes in the field.*

Pears strikes me as more measured, more level-headed than Britten. Holding so many patterns and lines of melody in his head must have made Britten a little strung-out. At least, that's what I imagine.

The more time I spend writing this, I realize that, more and more, I like to step away from the biographies and essays about Britten and Owen. The men exist so vividly in my imagination, now. One fact—a note about the weather, a cheerful salutation in a letter—can conjure an entire scene, an entire world in my mind. Spinning scenes out of nothing becomes easier the more I read and write. I feel as though I've seen their lives in my dreams.

OWEN GOES TO dinner one night at the Reform with H.G. Wells, author of *The Time Machine* and *The War of the Worlds*. Wells has kind eyes beneath upturned eyebrows that make him look perpetually worried. He tells Owen that the editor of *The Nation*, Henry William Massingham, has been talking of Owen's poem, "Miners." Wells himself heard of Owen from Massingham. Owen can barely eat his potatoes and beef stew. Editors are talking about him. Editors! And a prominent writer has sought him out! It was not so long ago that Owen sat by the front window of his childhood home, reading Keats and Shelley and only imagining his name in print.

A little more than a month later, in December of 1917, Owen receives a letter from a friend of Sassoon, another Great War poet named Robert Graves. "Don't make any mistake, Owen," Graves writes, "You are a fine poet already, & are going to be more so. I won't have the impertinence to criticize...Puff out your chest a little, and be big for you've more right than most of us...So outlive this war." When Owen receives this letter, he reads it again and again. All of the horrors of war, all of the drafts, the nightmares, the prayers left unsaid on his lips—they are worth something as long as he writes of them.

TO BE BACK in the damp and the gray and the fog—to be home. Britten can't discern his true feelings. He is, of course, thrilled to see his sisters and their families, and to return to his home at the Mill in Snape. But the rubble and destruction tear a chasm in him. When he was in America—writing, sunbathing, meeting new friends—was he truly being an artistic ambassador? Was he standing up for his country? Doing something good for this land and its people that are now desecrated and destined to rebuild for years to come? The people Britten passes in the street appear both crushed and ferocious, like gargoyles hunched over their church spires. They look protective and diminished at once.

Still, he knows that he could not have killed. When he applies at the London Tribunal to be listed as a Conscientious Objector, he speaks truthfully about his beliefs. He will compose and do his best to leave a legacy for England. He will do all he can, but he cannot pick up a gun and kill.

He writes on the Fourth of May in 1942:

Statement to the Local Tribunal for the Registration of Conscientious Objectors...

Since I believe that there is in every man the spirit of God, I cannot destroy.... The whole of my life has been devoted to acts of creation (being by profession a composer) and I cannot take part in acts of destruction...I believe sincerely that I can help my fellow human beings best, by continuing the work I am most qualified to do by the nature of my gifts and training, i.e. the creation or propagation of music...

—Benjamin Britten

He and Pears both apply and soon receive the responses in the mail. They officially become Conscientious Objectors and are now required to complete a number of compositions and performances in order to cement themselves as working artists whose art benefits England and the world.

With his letter in hand, Britten walks the halls of his beloved Mill toward the piano. The melodies in his head never cease, just quiet for a time. He lets them take over the space in his mind as he sits at the bench. His familiar clutter of pages and pencils are strewn about the piano; his metronome sits, dusty and waiting, at a small table beside him. He lays down the letter on top of one of the piles. His music is the reason for his exemption from war. It is a gift, a privilege.

The melodies come to him, key and time signatures writing themselves in his mind. His hands stretch once, twice, and set themselves on the cool keys. He plays a few chords, a few arpeggios and scales. His fingers warm, and he moves them faster across the keys. This—*this*—is his life.

I SIT IN bed with my computer open, the *Requiem* crackling over my tinny speakers. Britten's score sits open on my lap. With a finger, I follow the fast-moving measures as they explode and pass by. How did he write this? What did he see and hear when he notched a note into an eighth note? How did he make sense of these sharps and flats and naturals that pound and grind against each other? How did he know that this chaos was right?

So many people must have told him no. No, this doesn't make sense or, No, this won't work, or, Why don't you do something a little simpler, a little prettier, more easily recognized as elegiac? And he said no back.

When I listen to the *War Requiem* now, all it takes for me to gasp and cry is to imagine myself surrounded by the wall of sound that crashed over me when the orchestra played. The *Requiem* reaches a full *fortissimo*, a level of sound that I had never heard before in any piece of music. When I stood in the stands, the vibrations reverberated in my chest and I wouldn't have been able to hear my voice had I screamed. It was then I knew the power of a hundred-voice choir. If even ten voices were gone, the audience could not have heard us. Every single one of us needed to sing *forte*. We had to completely open up so as not to strain our voices. We had to sing and support the other voices and we had to let ourselves be supported by them. We had to trust that, together, we would be heard.

Now, when I hook up my speaker to my laptop and listen to the *Sanctus* or the *Libera Me,* if I picture the exact place I stood in the risers and imagine the shaking feeling in my chest as the sound waves moved through me, I can feel it again—that intense, painful, and surprising quake of realizing all that music can do.

IN NOVEMBER 1917, Owen receives a large envelope from *The Nation*. He climbs the hotel stairs quickly, his hands gently holding the edges of the envelope. When he enters his room, he stops for a moment to look around before crossing to his bed. Sunshine spills through the window and leaves long blocks of light across the floor. Outside, the ocean looks more blue than its usual gray. He sits down on the edge of the bed with the envelope on his lap, thankful that he should receive this package while still in the small room by the seaside that has become his home. Here, silence fills the room. No shells or shots interrupt the quiet, only the occasional rattle of the windowpane when a large gust of wind blows in off the sea. He can spend time in this moment.

He slides his finger beneath the flap and opens the envelope. The magazine slides onto his lap and he picks it up, feels its weight in his hands. He opens to his poem, "Miners," and brushes his finger across the byline. His name in print. His first publication in a national magazine.

I saw white bones in the cinder-shard,
Bones without number.
For many hearts with coal are charred,
And few remember.

Owen closes his eyes and remembers the day he wrote this poem from a trench. Wrote—his lips twitch into a smile—he scrawled it on the back of a letter to the editor. He could not keep the dirt from the paper. He is surprised they could read his handwriting at all.

And now here it is. In print. For all of England to see. He closes the magazine and rises from the bed's edge. Owen walks down to the hotel lobby in search of another envelope. He will send the magazine to his mother. She will read it and be proud of him. She will keep it safe.

AT MY KITCHEN table in Virginia, books rise in haphazard stacks around me and papers spill from tattered file folders, scattering themselves across the floor. Scribbled-on Post-its cover the tablecloth like confetti. The refrigerator hums, all the lights are on, and I read letters written by Benjamin Britten and Peter Pears. As I read, their faces, wrinkled with laughter, float up before me, and I hear their voices. Pears's voice is smooth and Britten's has a tad more gravel to it. He is, as those American *Times* writers wrote all those years ago "as English as rain." That's what he sounds like to me: rain.

Their correspondence has me laughing tonight. In June of 1942, Pears is away—singing, I presume—and Britten opens the letter by referring to their phone call. "My darling—It was so heavenly to hear your voice, a few minutes ago. But don't those blasted minutes shoot by? One never has time to say what one wants, but anyhow over that cold instrument one never could say what one wants."

Of course the telephone seemed cold to him. Britten and Pears lived in a world made warm by making music together. They felt the temperature of the room rise as they played and sang. They watched each other grow flushed. When Britten looked up from the piano, he would have seen the slight sheen of sweat on Pears's brow, courtesy of those demanding high notes he'd written for him.

He continues: "I do need you so desparately—I'm afraid I get such fits of depression when you're not around. I have been feeling all this beastly business so heavily on me recently, and the horrible loneliness—but I mustn't get sentimental, even if the radio is playing the Vltava!"

I smile at his misspellings, his dramatics. So he does get lonely, like I do. I slide my glasses to the top of my head and lean back to look at the photos I've taped to the wall. Chimes clang from somewhere outside and I feel my house creak as wind sweeps about its sides. Britten looks past me, serious and focused on something in the distance. I do not feel quite so alone anymore. I turn back to the letters. I keep reading.

ON A WINTER night in London, Britten sits in the Duke's Hall at the Royal Academy of Music for a concert in which Pears will sing with the Pro Canto Singers, a choir made up entirely of blind vocalists. The music, *St. Nicholas*, Britten's own composition, is a sweet song, and Pears always sings it wonderfully. Britten watches the way the choralists' fingers move across their scores. He listens to the music, to the sweep and cut of the voices as they travel octaves and fall down fifths and fourths in perfect harmony.

Pears takes deep breaths, his belly swelling, his face alight with music. Does he ever grow weary of singing Britten's compositions? Would he ever say so if he did? A quick flutter in Britten's chest—lucky, he is so lucky to have found a person who understands the music that lives in him and that he hears in everything: chimes on the side of the Amityville house were *pianissimo* in E, A, and C in the summer breeze. The dog that lives above them in their London flat has *forte* staccato barks. They—he and Pears—are an E major chord. Complex, round, complete.

It is winter, 2014, and it has been a while since I've read Owen's letters. I open the huge, celery-green book that's been sitting on my kitchen table for the past several months. I page through, looking for where I last left off and realize that I can locate myself in time more quickly than before. Last summer, I made cheat sheets of dates and places with markers on scraps of paper and hung them on my wall: "WWI or The Great War," I wrote, "28 July 1914—11 Nov 1918, 9 million combatants, 7 million civilians dead." I don't need to look at the reference sheets taped to my wall anymore. Over the course of the past year, this information has slowly seeped into my brain. When I find a passage that doesn't look familiar and check its date, I know it can't be what I'm looking for, because 1914 is too early; I want to read about after Craiglockhart. I'm in 1917 now.

1917. My grandfather would have been three years old.

There—I find it. A letter from Owen to Siegfried Sassoon. A letter from one friend to another. This letter is different in tone from the ones he writes to his mother. Those are loving, yes, but detached. The words written to Sassoon, on the other hand, seem to lift and swirl across the page. They are dreamy. In my mind, they are a deep violet—the moment after a vivid sunset, just before the world goes black. In the letter, Owen reminisces about his time at Craiglockhart with Sassoon and the friends they made, other broken soldiers rebuilding themselves.

"Someday," he writes, "I must tell how we sang, and how we laughed till the meteors showered around us, and we fell calm under the winter stars. And some of us saw the pathway of the spirits for the time. And seeing it so far above us, and feeling the good road so safe beneath us, we praised God with louder whistling; and knew we loved one another as no men love for long."

I try to conjure him here at my kitchen table. I imagine trying to talk to him. I imagine saying: "Your writing—" and then I imagine the breath being swept right out of me and up through my roof and into the stars. There is nothing I can say to describe the beauty of those lines, how devastating it is that such lines would not be written by him for much longer, how wonderful and miraculous it is that these lines exist at all. I feel all of that, all at once, every time I read a word by him.

When I walked outside today, the sun inched toward the horizon and the world looked pink. I have been alone all day, but haven't felt so.

IN JULY OF 1945, a month after the opening of his opera *Peter Grimes*, Britten goes to Germany with American violinist Yehudi Menuhin to perform at the Bergen-Belsen Displaced Persons Camps. Three months prior, in April of 1945, Canadian and British forces arrived at Bergen-Belsen to find 13,000 unburied bodies and 60,000 people suffering from typhoid, tuberculosis, dysentery, and starvation in a camp that was built to hold 10,000 people. In the months following Liberation, 10,000 more survivors of Bergen-Belsen died from their lingering illnesses and ailments, on average 500 people a day from that camp alone. Between 1941 and 1945 over eleven million people had been killed by Nazi Germany in mass shootings, pogroms, and across all concentration camps.

Survivors had been relocated to a nearby German army camp that was now known as the Bergen-Belsen Displaced Persons Camp. Britten and Menuhin play in a designated music room where concerts and dance performances are often put on by visiting artists and displaced persons themselves. The entertainment is an effort to bring joy and distraction to the survivors as they wait for the chaotic aftermath of the war to die down. Britten tries to settle himself deep inside the music, to play in such a way that the survivors' suffering, however briefly, will lift from their hearts and minds. After the performance, when he walks around the camp, he is struck by their bodies, their thin skin stretched over violent angles, their hollowed-out and hungry eyes. He does not understand how bodies like this can still be living. He does not understand how people can do this to one another.

I GET AN email informing me that the fifth volume of *The Selected Letters of Benjamin Britten* has arrived for me at my library from a large university. I get in my car and drive straight over. I've been waiting for this volume: years 1958-1965, the years in which Britten is commissioned for the *War Requiem*, writes it, and conducts it at the Coventry Cathedral. The librarians are used to handing me these large black books—each one has around 1000 pages of letters and footnotes. I carry the book back to my car and quickly page through it. The pages' corners are not rounded from wear or use. No pencil marks, no left-behind Post-its, no dog-eared creases. I smell the pages and conclude that this book is brand new.

When I get home, I turn to the Index of Correspondents. I recognize names. Some of them I've met in Britten's earlier letters: Barbara and Robert Britten, Elizabeth Mayer. Others I know because of their fame: Dmitri Shostakovich, Aaron Copland, and E.M. Forster. And then, toward the bottom of the list I see Galina Vishnevskaya, the Russian soprano soloist of the *War Requiem*. I know her voice so well, have said her name to myself so many times, looked at her picture online while I listen to her solos.

I flip to the next page where a note on Britten's spelling appears. The editors write that for the majority of the letters, the misspellings have been corrected. "We have occasionally retained a mis-spelling," they write, "but only when it adds something to the character and flavor of what Britten was writing or provokes a smile." This last bit makes me smile down to the page and make a mental note to write a letter to Donald Mitchell, Philip Reed, and Mervyn Cooke, the editors. To know that there are people out there who love Britten as much as or more than I do, gives me a feeling similar to meeting one of my best friend's best friends: surely, I will grow fond of this person as you have, because I am so fond of you.

Sometimes I feel so small and alone in my house, typing away at something so huge and complicated and, perhaps, strange. But the books of letters on my desk assure me that I am not alone or small. I have access to hundreds of letters that Britten wrote to over a hundred different people. The brief encounters, the passionate relationships, the disagreements, and shared triumphs contained in his life fly through my fingers as I turn the pages.

I open at random to the middle of the book and see a copy of a scrawled poem as part of a footnote for Letter 1038. I recognize the handwriting, but it is not Britten's—it is Owen's. The title: "Anthem for Dead Youth." From the title I know that this is an early draft. Drops of ink stain the bottom of the page and about a third of the lines are heavily crossed out. I read the editor's note: "One of Wilfred Owen's many drafts for 'Anthem for Doomed Youth,' given to Britten by the poet's brother, Harold."

"What?" I ask the pages. How could I not have known this? To know that Owen's brother gave Britten a draft of one of Owen's most famous poems makes me close my eyes and press my hands to my chest. Britten held a draft that Owen wrote forty-five years before in 1917, one year before he died along the Sambre-Oise Canal. Now, almost a hundred years after Owen wrote the draft and over fifty years since Britten first held it in his hands, there is a young woman in a small house in Virginia learning of this connection and putting her head in her hands. Knowing this makes her feel full and expansive. Knowing this reminds her that there is no end to the depths of connections we make in this world, whether we recognize them or not.

I feel as though I've taken a bite of dessert before dinner. I have more to learn about Britten and his commission for the *War Requiem* before I will let myself read the letters he wrote while composing the work. I stick a blue Post-it beside Owen's handwriting and flip back to 1958.

On October 7, 1958, John Lowe, British radio producer, conductor, and Artistic Director of the 1962 Coventry Cathedral Festival, wrote a letter to Britten expressing the Festival's desire to commission from him a work for orchestra and chorus. "The new work they seek could be full length or a substantial 30-40 minutes one: its libretto could be sacred or secular...The Committee will be very pleased if this great occasion could help bring forth an important new work from you...they will be v. pleased if you would conduct it."

The next day Britten wrote back: "Would you please tell the Arts Committee at Coventry how touched I was by their kind invitation to write something for the consecration of the new Cathedral in 1962. I should very much like to undertake this...Seriously, I should be very honoured to be connected with such a significant and moving occasion, and shall do my best to turn out something worthy of it."

When I read these words, my breath catches. Here is the beginning: this quick exchange over two days started the composition of the *War Requiem*. Over the course of the next four years, Britten would compose the piece that many regard as the most important work of his life.

I look over Britten's composition sketches in the following pages. Drawn in haste, each sharp and flat decorates the page in different ways. Whole staffs are scribbled over, decrescendos fold in on themselves, and dotted half notes and quarter notes float above curling stems. It's messy, imperfect. But from these sketches comes beauty, ugliness, art.

ALTHOUGH IT'S FEBRUARY, 1959, the soft breeze feels spring-like and Britten takes a walk down to the river near his home in Suffolk. The river ripples blue beneath the swans and shell-ducks, the cormorants and lapwings. Britten walks alongside it, breathing in the warm air and counting with his steps the days until Pears returns from touring in Canada.

The river water looks like velvet. Britten leans over in an attempt to see beneath the surface, but he only spots the shadow of his head marking the water a deeper blue. He is forty-six years old. He has written ten operas including *Peter Grimes, The Turn of the Screw, Noye's Fludde,* and *Gloriana*, an opera composed for the coronation of Queen Elizabeth II. They all received rave reviews and have gone on many tours around England and America. Just this past year, he composed an orchestral song cycle titled *Nocturne,* Op. 60 that was performed by Pears and the BBC Symphony Orchestra at the Leeds Festival. The work blended poetry by eight English poets including Keats, Shelley, Shakespeare, Tennyson, and Owen. With the *Nocturne* and with every composition, he challenges himself to create boundary-pushing work that will engage listeners on multiple levels. He has composed symphonies, concertos, quartets, duets, and choral pieces. He has made countless recordings with the BBC and Decca. He no longer gets nervous to appear on television. He is, quite simply, famous.

And yet.

Britten stares down into his shadow on the surface of the water. He searches the darkness, trying to see whatever swims, floats, or sinks below. This is not all he is. His work, while rewarding and important, is not enough.

He has found gray hair sprouting at his temples. He has bags beneath his eyes that will never go away. His body is growing older, but musically he is just entering his prime. Every composition, every note written, hummed aloud, scratched out, and rewritten has been building toward something.

He and Pears have sketched out their schedules for the next few years. First, the Aldeburgh Festival, then a few more commissions, a tour or two for Pears, perhaps another opera, and the Coventry commission.

The Coventry commission. Britten straightens and looks out across the river to the trees that will bloom fierce greens come spring. The ducks and swans spin circles on the river. He has always loved England, and yet, when bombs exploded the Coventry Cathedral, he was in America. When people were starving and toiling and being killed in concentration camps, he had abandoned his home. He was not there to work to make a difference or even to bear witness. But so many others did.

Looking at the river, he thinks of Wilfred Owen, a poet whose work he's recently encountered. He wrote of the horrors of war—the pity of war. Britten had paged through a collection of his poetry before finding "The Kind Ghosts," the Owen poem he had set in the *Nocturne.* The melodic lines he had written for the piece were smooth and haunting, floating over increasingly distraught strums of the strings. To use "The Kind Ghosts" had been an easy choice—*Nocturne* was all about sleep and dreams and twilit moments before wakefulness. But Owen had written so many other gruesome, unflinching lines of verse. The pity of war. Britten speaks the words aloud and listens to the way they cut through the air before being swallowed by the sound of the river. He waits for a moment, and then turns and walks back toward home—determined and hopeful, sure that something—something powerful—is unfurling within him.

EVERY DAY THAT passes by, Owen feels he is heading both closer to and farther from understanding the ultimate truth he seeks: what is war but ceaseless, pointless death? Why do people insist that war is the way to solve problems? Owen sits in his turreted room at the hotel and looks down at the sea stretching wide before him. He begins a letter to his mother and thinks back to last winter, when he was freezing in French trenches. The land had stretched bare before him. Desecrated, empty. Before the war, maples and oaks must have stood there, shading long grasses, butterflies, and rabbits. Wildflowers must have spread across the hills and hollows, back when the land naturally undulated, back before shells and explosions rewrote the ground.

In France, the men he leaned beside in the trenches had ghostly faces. They looked as if they'd been submerged in water for a long, long, time, and, at the sound of a large boom, had surfaced, already defeated, always afraid.

He does not want to go back to the front lines. He thinks of Sassoon. Sassoon, who left and then came back to the war. In the end, Sassoon could not desert his fellow men. He must be back in France already.

A year ago tonight, Owen was awake in his wind-shaken tent in the middle of a vast encampment, so different from the drafty but still warm hotel where he now writes. He looks out the window, pen still in hand, and remembers the sound of the Scottish troops that camped around him, troops who are now dead.

Owen closes his eyes and pictures the looks on their faces. "It was not despair, or terror," he writes to his mother, "it was more terrible than terror, for it was a blindfold look, and without expression, like a dead rabbit's. It will never be painted, and no actor will ever seize it. And to describe it, I think I must go back and be with them."

Owen pauses and looks down at the words he has written in ink. He will send them to his mother and she will keep them. She will keep them for as long as he lives and after. He breathes deeply and looks out to the dark sea before writing again: "We are sending seven officers straight out tomorrow. I have not said what I am thinking this night, but next December I will surely do so.

I know what you are thinking, and you know me—Wilfred."

By next December, Owen will be dead.

4. SANCTUS

"Pleni sunt ceoli et terra Gloria tua..."

"Heaven and earth are full of thy glory..."

OUTSIDE, THICK FLAKES of snow pelted themselves at the ground. Muddy water pooled on the stands around our boots. Dr. A told us to open our scores to the *Sanctus*. "This movement starts with the soprano soloist. She sings with the bells, cymbals, and glockenspiel. Rehearsal score eighty-five, that's when we come in," said Dr. A. He stood behind the piano, his giant score spread out on top. "This is where you throw out everything you know about choral singing. Do not try to blend; in fact, try not to blend. Make sure that you spit out the line '*pleni sunt coeli et terra Gloria tua*' at a completely different pace and time than those on either side of you. Chaos. Cacophony. That is what we want." He raised an arm toward the basses and gave them their pitch. Tentative and nervous, the basses whispered the Latin with wide, loose mouths. They sounded terrible. "Okay, okay, we still need articulation of consonants and unity of vowels even if we are not in unison," Dr. A said. "Tighten up. Let's all try this together."

I planted my feet a little wider apart and took a deep breath. Dr. A punched the keys and I picked out the top note of the eight-note chord. He pointed at us and we spoke the words on our pitches. We weren't singing, not really. I could hear my voice above Candice's and Liz's and winced. I sounded reedy, breathy, uncertain. Sometimes when singing the *Requiem*, I wondered if I was actually losing skill as a singer. Surely, this work strengthened my technique and ability to read music, but the actual sounds I produced, unlike those when I sang Brahms or simple hymns, weren't pretty. Measure to measure, my voice went from a barely audible whisper to a forceful *forte* charged with anger.

"*Pleni sunt coeli et terra Gloria tua,*" I sang-spoke. I tried not to listen to the other sopranos around me, but I could hear all of us accenting the same spots, drawing out the same vowels, creating the same crescendo-decrescendo arc we had learned so well over the past three years in choir.

Dr. A made his left hand into a fist. We stopped singing. He looked at us with a smile. "You have to undo what you've learned. You can go back to that in a few pages, I promise."

The bodies beside me tensed. I sensed the stifled sighs. So much of what we learned and did in college had a clear pattern and purpose. We followed a syllabus for each class. We plugged numbers into formulas. We wrote papers with thesis statements. Even in choir, we practiced our scales every day. We built on top of the basics. *Do-Re-Mi-Fa-So-La-Ti-Do. Do-Mi* was a third. *Do-So* a fifth. Major versus minor. We cupped our vowels with our lips. We put hands on our bellies and learned how to breathe.

Now, Dr. A told us to forget all of that. "Don't put an arc in your phrases. It should be almost mechanical, robotic. Crescendo the entire time. A steady, driving crescendo will lead us to the *Hosannahs* coming up. Try again."

I rolled my shoulders back and tried to forget the messiness, the inadequacy, the rules we had to break. Soon, Dr. A told us, we wouldn't flinch with surprise at the chaos we created. Soon we would know these Latin words like our own names. So for now, I tried to let go. This piece, these sounds—these were not things I could control. All I could do was let my diaphragm drop, push out my consonants and let the notes form in the spaces between them. All I could do was my best, nothing more.

OWEN SMOOTHES HIS hands across the paper. Soon, he will be back outside or in a tent, squatting down to write poems on crumpled sheets he rubs against his thigh to unwrinkle. But now, in this moment, he is at a small table with a chair. He looks through the window at the outside world and breathes deeply, relishing this quiet moment. He picks up his pen and lets his eyes gaze at the page though he is seeing something else. A quiet space. A still space. Weak light blurs the darkness away just enough that one can see a figure stirring awake.

He writes:

It seemed that out of battle I escaped
Down some profound dull tunnel, long since scooped
Through granites which titanic wars had groined.

Around the figure, other soldiers lie unmoving. In Owen's mind, they are the same dull and dusty colors as the walls of stone that contain them. The silence presses against the soldiers, so different than the blasting, quaking, moaning final battles from which they came. It is in this space—this quiet realm of Hell—where the soldier will meet the man he killed.

How many times had Owen imagined a meeting like this? How many men had he seen killed by another? How many men had he killed himself? How anyone who killed could remain alive and bear it would be a mystery until he himself awoke after death. He imagines the faces of the two soldiers meeting in his poem. Both young, both free of blood and bruises, both with eyes that had looked upon so many things—trees and birds and children and friends—with kindness. With love and awe. He will have the first soldier greet the other.

"Strange friend…here is no cause to mourn."
"None," said the other, "save the undone years,
The hopelessness. Whatever hope is yours,
Was my life also…"

Owen writes until, finally, he sets down the pen and leans back in the chair. He looks at the poem, his hands on either side of it. Do the words he's written, black ink on white paper, capture the blood gone cold in death? Has he contained life and life lost in this page? He looks at his fingers, long and slender, the tips of them just the tiniest bit cold in the chill of the room. He looks at his curling scrawl, the scribbled-out sections, the scratched-out words, the new additions cramped in the spaces between lines. It isn't finished. He reads through it again. He picks up his pen. It hovers above the final line. Tentatively, he writes so lightly that it looks like a question across the page.

"Let us sleep now. . . ."

That is all he wants for his soldiers. A peaceful, endless sleep. A forgetting of the pity that came before. And ahead of them only dreams.

Now WHEN I read *Letters from a Life*, I hear an orchestra tuning up as I turn the pages from May to August 1960. Britten has written letters to colleagues and friends explaining that he cannot take on work from 1960 through the winter of 1961 because he has "a big piece for Coventry" to do. Leonard Bernstein wrote to Britten asking if he would be one of "ten internationally prominent composers" to write a major work for the New York Philharmonic's inaugural 1961-1962 season, but Britten declined even that significant invitation. In a letter to music critic and the BBC Controller of Music, William Glock, Britten writes: "I have…got, as you know, this big commission for Coventry, a full evening's choral work, which I am absorbed in planning, & very much want now to have my mind clear to think about."

The editors of *Letters from a Life* insert "*War Requiem*" in brackets after the word "Coventry" when it appears in these early letters. The fact that Britten has not yet named the work thrills me. I cannot wait to watch it all unfold in his own words. He is setting the stage. He is preparing to begin. I wonder if he is nervous. He has a year and a half to write a piece for the new Coventry Cathedral. A year and a half to write a masterpiece.

OWEN TAKES FORTY-EIGHT hours leave, but only stops at home for a short time en route to London. There, he attends the wedding of his new friend Robert Graves. The wedding takes place at St. James's Piccadilly, and when Owen walks into the church, he realizes that the event is a rather small affair. People rest comfortably in the pews with space between them. Owen sits toward the back. It has been so long since he's been in a church. He slides his hand along the dark oak pew and breathes in that church smell that never changes no matter the church. The white ceilings dome above his head and sunlight glints off the gold molding that decorates the vaults. At the front of the church, six large panels of stained glass depict the Bible stories he once knew so well. He closes his eyes to images of Jesus, Mary, and the saints, and he wonders if he should pray. People continue to shuffle into the church. The moment passes. He opens his eyes.

A man in a very long coat and a very tall hat passes by him and sits in a pew a few rows ahead. He looks like a dandy from the 1870s, complete with wispy side whiskers and a walking stick. When the man turns his head to see the back of the church, Owen recognizes him: George Belcher, the artist and caricaturist, looking like a caricature himself. Excited, Owen continues to search for people he recognizes. He sees another famous caricaturist and novelist, Max Beerbohm, whose fairly recent collection of parodies, *A Christmas Garland*, had been well received and pointed toward his being of another level of genius. He also spots the publisher William Heinemann, Winston Churchill's Private Secretary named Edward Marsh, and the Scottish writer and translator C.K. Scott Moncrieff. Owen folds his hands tightly in his lap. The talents and energies of these people seem to buzz about the room. And to think—he is a published poet. Not all of these people would know his name, but, maybe, some do.

The murmurs cease when Robert Graves takes his place at the front. The organ begins sounding throughout the nave. The bride, Nancy Nicholson, walks down the aisle toward her groom. Owen doesn't pay much attention to the wedding ceremony. Instead, he thinks of the writers and artists who sit just meters away from him. Some of them have fought or fight still in the war, he knows, but many of them are free to make art and live as they please. A strange feeling settles in Owen's chest. His experiences in war have made him the poet he is, and yet, a life continually punctured by shells and blasts and bayonets is no life. But the destruction of war has been the making of him. What would he be doing, what would he be writing, if he hadn't enlisted in the Great War? He cannot fathom the man he'd be without it.

After the wedding, the guests join the bride and groom at a reception at Apple-Tree Yard at St. James's Square. There, Graves introduces him as "Owen, the poet." He shakes everyone's hands and tries to appear calm. Owen, the poet. He smiles all afternoon.

TODAY I READ *Letters From a Life* over tea in my kitchen. Cold air wafts in beneath the door to my porch and I tuck my feet beneath me. I read letters back and forth between Britten and cellist Mstislav Rostropovich as they plan a recital together, their correspondence translated between Russian and English. Letter after letter, Rostropovich continues to request that Britten compose a cello sonata for him. Britten agrees. In a letter from November 1960 he writes to Rostropovich:

> Of course you must know before making this decision what my piece will be like. I have been planning this very thoroughly in my head (I always go to the paper at a very late date); it will not be a long work, and I feel inclined to call it not a sonata but a Sonatina, or some qualified name. The movements will be short and there may be five or six. I am enjoying thinking about it enormously, especially with your lovely playing in mind. I hope I shall not go too far in exploiting the technique of the instrument, knowing that you can play anything!

Reading this passage of the letter excites me; finally, I receive a clue as to how Britten goes about composing pieces. I have read so often about times he felt blocked from his work, or days when music flowed from him freely, but I have not yet come across descriptions of his composing techniques. I am curious and keep a growing list of questions as I read through his letters and biographies: Does the melody or setting come first? Does he know immediately which instruments will take which melodic lines? How much revising does he do? Now, from this one small passage tucked into a letter to his friend, I understand that Britten begins with a lot of thinking in a way that is both abstract and concrete, precise and vague. I imagine him turning a melody over in his mind, tweaking and refining it, humming it under his breath as he goes for walks around the Red House. I can see him sit down at the piano and play a few chords before reaching for a pen and sketching the opening, there at the piano.

I continue reading about Rostropovich and learn that he was married to Galina Vishnevskaya, the Russian soprano soloist who sang in the original 1963 recording of the *War Requiem*. I am getting closer now. The composition swirling in the back of Britten's mind is starting to take shape. The players and the singers emerge onto the scene of his life. The elements of the *War Requiem* begin to thread together, and I watch as if from the wings. Sometimes I almost feel as if I were a part of it, as if I were there.

A MONTH AFTER Graves's wedding, Owen is still in Scarborough. He stands in the hotel's basement, shining his boots with a buff and rag. The latest rumor is that he will be sent to train with Light Duty Commanders in preparation for a return to the front. He has gotten used to the army life—the uniform, the orders, and the fear. He has gotten used to it, but he doesn't like it. When he receives orders to pack up and move on to another place, he feels acutely that he is a dispensable pawn at the mercy of the cold cogs and gears that make up the machinery of government. The men who sit in conference rooms and push figurines across a map— all they see are the numbers, the blunt facts. To them, war is cold. War is duty. Do they not know that war is hot and burning? Owen buffs his boots with more vigor. He slaps the rag across the shining toes.

They don't understand that war is the rotting hand jutting out from the trench wall, the dead man behind the hand, his face forgotten. They don't understand that war is the blood spilling from his friend's lips while he sinks to his knees, the blood steaming in the snow, the snow bright as spring cherries. War is the yellowed ankles, the purpled feet, the blackened toes, the walking on dead feet for miles. War is his friend blown to pieces before his eyes—all those stories, memories, and dreams that his friend kept locked inside, lost forever. In their stead, the red pulp of a body no longer a body.

Abruptly, Owen drops the rag and his boots on the table and runs outside in his bare feet. He heads for the sea. The salty air and continual fog have melted the snow, and Owen walks toward the rocky shorelines on soggy grass. He staggers toward the water without thinking. It is difficult to breathe and his hands clutch at his coat lapels, holding desperately onto himself. When he steps into the freezing water, he gasps and shudders.

Owen looks out across the gray North Sea. Somewhere, thousands of kilometers away, America rises out of a different ocean. South America, too. The icy water numbs Owen's feet. He wishes that he could numb his entire body and mind. He doesn't want to feel this war anymore. He doesn't want to feel this fear.

Still standing in the water, Owen turns around and looks at the hotel where he has lived and worked and written for the past three months. He has grown fond of Scarborough and his life here. He does not want to leave, but now it seems he must.

On unfeeling feet, he walks away from the gray sea and back toward the hotel.

It is strange to read unflattering letters or come across rumors about Britten in articles I find online. I never know what to do with the information. Of course people aren't perfect. Of course people are not universally well-liked. The portrait I've drawn in my mind is rosy-toned, soft around the edges. There must be reasons for some of the shadows about the eyes, the downturned lip, but I have not wanted to see them.

Today, I read in one of his biographies that Britten had what many called his "corpses," friends who did something to offend him, and who were consequently frozen out of his life. This seems a harsh thing to do, but when I think about it, it appears true; I have watched Wystan Auden's name drop out of the letters. When a reference to him appears every other year or so, it is in the form of a slight. I read about other people who have joined the ranks of the corpses. One was a soprano named Sophie Wyss. I remember reading about her. She had been the original soloist for Britten's *Les Illuminations* before he replaced her with Pears. Their friendship had ended after that because Britten did not find her talent to be at the level he would have liked. Eric Crozier appears on the list and I recognize his name from recent letters; he worked with Britten on the hit opera *Peter Grimes*. Now I know that before too long he will be cast aside by the composer. These are not the only names. Britten seems to have been a fickle friend. Some biographers defend him, saying that he was a brilliant composer who could only surround himself with like-minded, highly ambitious, hard-working people. They say that he did not have time for the lazy or the petty.

Of course, when I read these claims, my first instinct is to agree with the biographers and to take Britten's side. When Britten makes a joke about Auden in a letter to Pears, I am amused. Or, when I read a review in one of America's papers about Britten's harsh rehearsals, I justify Britten's rudeness. He wrote the music, I argue to no one; he knows how it is supposed to sound.

But then there are nights like tonight, when I lean back from my kitchen table and stare at the stern face that I've taped to my wall. Britten's eyebrows are pushed down. A slight frown falls into shadow. His tie is perfectly knotted. He looks like a serious composer. He also looks difficult. Maybe even a little mean. Perhaps he had to be so intense in order to give rise to such important music. I will never know for sure. I am forced to grapple with the fact that, despite how close I feel to him, I will never truly know Britten.

When the *Sanctus* opened up from the mismatched chanting, we sang notes that stretched long and opened our throats. The sopranos split into three parts and sang "*Hosannah*" in a major triad above everyone else. We sang operatic, vibrato-full notes. Beside me, Liz sounded like the opera singer she aimed to be after graduation. "You can really open up here," said Dr. A. "The orchestra will be doing their own thing, and you'll be singing against cymbals and strings on the off-beat. You have to stay strong on your part."

This was the kind of singing we were used to: clear harmonies, chords in major triads, enough going on in all the voice parts that the sopranos could let go a little and make our *forte* an actual *forte*, instead of the *mezzo-forte* we usually sang to keep balance. Even though this was the most accessible part of the *Requiem* we had yet come across, there were still facets that made the movement strange. We sang a counterpoint to the orchestra. Each section split itself into three or four vocal parts. Perhaps most disturbing, we sensed—somehow—that this "simplicity" of choral scoring would later break down into something insane and complex and overwhelming. Each new flip of the page brought a flood of adrenaline to my chest. To learn the *Requiem* was to learn that you never knew what was coming next. To learn the *Requiem* was to learn that you had to do things that appeared impossible. I looked up from my score, made eye contact with Dr. A and felt my lips form a smile around the note I sang. I was doing the impossible.

AFTER A RAINY summer of resting an aching wrist, Britten agonizes over all the time spent waiting. Waiting to play the piano. Waiting to compose. When Pears leaves to sing in Dartington Hall alongside renowned pianist Maria Curcio, Britten decides to meet him there. They spend a few days and then drive through the continuous rain to visit their friends. On their way home, they stop at the Coventry Cathedral to see the work that has been done on its restoration and rebuilding. When they drive up, they see a very modern-looking brick building connected to the remaining shell of the spire and the roofless ruins. Soon, a garden will sprout brightly colored flowers and people will be walking in and around the grounds. When Britten and Pears enter the new building next to the ruins, they tilt their heads up to the honeycomb of scaffolding near the ceiling. Britten finds it difficult to determine what the space will actually be like, because so much of the building is still underway. He walks toward one of the back walls, which is covered in some sort of concrete stucco.

He gives Pears a withering look. This material—what so many supposed experts call "acoustic"—will only suck up and dry out sound.

Britten circles the rest of the cathedral and then walks outside, stopping between the ruins and the new St. Michael's Cathedral. The sun warms his face. He thinks of the soldiers and civilians who had felt this same warmth from the constant sun before they died in the war. He takes a deep breath and closes his eyes. People are killed, countries are broken, faiths are left behind, and yet it is that beautiful thing in human nature—resilience—which keeps beauty coming at every turn. When Britten opens his eyes, he sees a bird arise from the top of the spire and fly off into the blue.

ON MARCH 12, 1918, the military sends Owen to Ripon, England, for training in preparation for a return to the front lines. The state of the camp terrifies him. Shoddy huts filled with rubbish and dirt hold too many men for any semblance of comfort. Owen tries to clear a space on the ground for his pack and sleeping mat and hopes that no mice find their way into his belongings.

Early the next morning, the men wake and begin their drills. After months of repose in Craiglockhart and Scarborough, Owen's shell shock has improved, but now his body feels heavy and uncontrollable. His arms cannot support his own weight for long when he does push-ups, and when the men run in endless circles around the barren fields of the camp, Owen stops often to catch his breath. The commanders rank the men based on their sprints and exercises and then place them in a level one through six. After his first week of training, Owen discovers that he is in the sixth level, the lowest, but he is not the only one.

When they retire to their cramped huts at night, Owen listens to the men breathing from their cots. They have all been broken. Not one of them takes falling asleep for granted.

I AM NEARING the end of Wilfred Owen's *Collected Letters*. Many months ago, when the book seemed too long and the volume of letters inside insurmountable, I plowed through months' worth of letters in hours at a time. Owen wrote a letter to his mother practically every day. I thought I would never run out of letters to read. Now, I have only fifty-eight letters left. I have read 615, the earliest dating from 1898 when Owen was five years old. "my dear mother," the letter reads, "i no that you have got there safely. We are making huts. I have got a latern, and we are lighting them up to-night. With love from Wilfred I remain your loving son Wilfred."

These letters end with the ending of a life. At the time that I write this, Wilfred Owen has been dead for almost a hundred years, and yet, in this space I've created, where I read and write about him, he is still alive. He is looking out his window in the Clifton Hotel, wondering where he'll be sent next. He is struggling through push-ups and drills and counting down the hours until he can make sense of his experiences on paper. He is signing letters to his mother and friends. He is taking off his boots and socks and rubbing his feet. He is waking and watching the first pink rays of morning ease up the sky. When I reach the last letter and read the last words that he wrote to his loved ones—what will I do? How will I feel?

Unlike the recipients of Owen's letters in this book, I know that he dies on November 4, 1918. From where I am right now in the *Collected Letters*, I have six months left with him. 187 days. Fifty-eight letters that he wrote over the course of those last months.

I don't want these letters to end. While I'm still learning his story, he is still alive to me in some way. I can picture how he looks in uniform, how his hair falls on his forehead, how he walks with purpose through the halls of the hotel and the camp at Ripon. I don't want to picture him going down. I don't want to see him fall beside a river, shot through with bullets. I don't want to see his blood, the way his eyes go wide, then dark.

I don't want him to die.

But he is already dead.

I know this. I have known this from the beginning and still I put my head down on my kitchen table and I cry.

I cannot read any more letters tonight.

THE REQUESTS FOR commissions keep arriving by mail and by telegraph and Britten says no to all of them. This—the *War Requiem*—will be one of the most important compositions of his life. With the scale and the subject, it could be no other way. Britten starts with the libretto. He sits with his piano in sight, his large notebooks from his Lowestoft days spread before him, his copy of Owen's poetry collection perched across one palm, a pencil in the other. He underlines and circles and stars lines of Owen's poetry, poetry that reaches out from the page across time and clutches the reader by the throat. Poetry that demands a reckoning. Poetry that denounces war and honors those who gave their lives to it in the same breath. He wants to join Owen's words with the Latin Mass for the Dead to create a complex, layered piece that defies categorization.

Throughout the planning process, Britten takes long walks, he writes in his diary, he sits before windows, he stands on the beach, and, always, he thinks about the words whirling through his mind. Ideas come to him in bright flashes, and he waits to see which ones stick. A tenor soloist and a baritone soloist. A soprano soloist, a choir, the Latin Mass. A boys' choir. Organ. A chamber orchestra. He knows that there are many ideas right now. He sits down at the circular table in his studio and writes down the ideas and looks at them, waiting for the moment when he will cross some out and make the project simpler, more direct. He stares at the notebook.

He flips to a new page and draws a line down the middle. On the left side, he will write the words for the Latin Mass for the Dead and on the right side he will write the Owen poems he decides to use. When he begins transcribing the poems, he can hear the music carry the words as he reads each line. "What passing bells for these who die as cattle?" He hears the rise of the tenor voice, the abrupt fall, and then the whistling of the woodwinds catching him. "Only the stuttering rifle's rapid rattle can patter out their hasty orisons." He hears the snare drumming in a sharp rhythm below the voice.. He strikes his pencil against the bottom of the page in short bursts: an eighth note here, a quarter rest there, another eighth note. Perhaps he will change his mind later when he goes to draft the work, but he has a suspicion that he will not.

The lyrics begin arranging themselves in his mind. Owen's "Anthem for Doomed Youth" will begin it all with the *Requiem Aeternam*. The poem "Strange Meeting" will come at the end and be interwoven with the *Libera Me*. Britten writes in who will sing which parts as he hears them: soprano soloist, tenor, baritone, boys' choir, chorus. Not all of the notes are clear in his mind; he cannot distinguish them just yet. The sections exist more as key and time signatures and emotions that wash over different sections. Gradually, they will harden into notes and melodies.

Britten sits back and taps the notebook with his pen, looking at what he has written so far. How to make it all fit? How to make it flow? Britten worries, wonders if it is possible to link together two such different pieces of writing. But are they really that different from one another? They both deal with death, with judgment, with struggle. He can make the piece itself sound like a struggle—he might have to in order to make everything fit and work together. He has always been on the experimental side of modern compositions, but, he suspects, this will push the boundaries of what he has done and what has yet to be done in modern classical music history. Someone has to write something like this—this, *this*, whatever this will be—and why shouldn't it be him? He will just have to be brave. All he needs is a fraction of the bravery Owen had.

The blocks of text start to organize themselves in his mind and he draws arrows and circles around some of the words. The tenor and baritone soloists. Voices of soldiers. They will sing the lines of English poetry. The soprano and the choir will sing the Latin Mass for the Dead. The work will be written in fractures, the musicians divided into parts. It will be disjointed, dysfunctional, the embodiment of war. The music will be dissonant throughout, but then everything will come together at the very end. The resolution—a major triad—a hope for peace.

Everything else in the world diminuendos and Britten lets himself fall into the great wave of music being born.

OWEN FIDDLES WITH his pen and curls the edges of the paper against his fingertips. He presses the pen to the paper and watches the trail of ink he leaves on the page. His words fall into formation: line after line after line, but they take their time as they knock about and meander their way from his mind to the page. He shapes the words in his mouth as he writes. "Deeper sleep," "winds' scimitars," "thin and sodden head." He feels reckless in the moment he decides to break a line—it is as if he were leaping off a rocky cliff to blue waters below. The next line catches him. He finds his footing in the poem once again and lays down another pathway of words. "His hair being one with the grey grass." Another line break, another leap—"And finished fields of autumns that are old…"

On the page he can take risks that do not put his life in peril. His words cannot kill, unlike those written orders that send him from battlefield to battlefield, each step closer to the front lines—a flirtation with death. When he dives headlong into a new stanza, he relishes the unknown that waits to be uncovered on the page. It is so unlike the unknowns of his daily life as a soldier. Where will he be sent next? Will this be the last letter he writes and sends? Though he writes of war in his poetry, the very act of writing is in direct opposition to the destructive forces of guns and cannons and blasts and shells. He is a creator, working word by word to right the tilted, gruesome world that seems so bent on decimating as much life as possible.

I FIND COPIES of pages from Britten's notebook in *Letters from a Life* and I read the draft of the libretto for the *War Requiem.* Arrows and boxes crowd his slanted script, but the pages appear orderly. Not much is crossed out. His choices for text and text order seem sure. I search for signs of self-doubt in the writing and the notes in the margins, but find none. How long did it take him to sort all of this out? His talent in composition, though at times wild and experimental, was not questioned by his contemporaries. Every key change, every dynamic marking, every fermata and glissando, has purpose. Nothing is gratuitous or forced. Every note hangs together in a delicate web.

I flip a page in *Letters from a Life* and I see the title of the fifth section: "My Subject is War, February 1961—July 1962." I pause. I have read 1002 letters written by Britten leading up to this composition and these years of his life, but suddenly I don't feel ready.

I close my eyes and imagine my place between Candice and Liz in the soprano section of Chapel Choir. I try to remember the feel of the cranberry robes we wore, the stole with white silk lining that always slid off one shoulder. I feel the heat of the other bodies around me. I hear them breathing. I hear their voices.

I open my eyes. I turn the page.

5. AGNUS DEI

"Agnus Dei, qui tollis peccata mundi, dona eis requiem."

"Lamb of God, who takes away the sins of the world, grant them rest."

OUTSIDE ST. OLAF's music building, the snow melted in an unexpected early thaw that spring of 2013. We knew the warm weather would not last and that the snow would be back, so we stayed outside until the last possible minute before dashing in to grab our music folders and find our places on the risers. One Friday during the thaw, I stood outside with Candice and shared a cookie from the campus café before choir. We had shrugged off our coats and let the sun touch our bare skin. "Winter will come back for sure," she said, "but just think: the next time the weather feels like this, we'll be performing the *Requiem*. Then we'll be graduating."

"I can think about graduating," I said, "but I can't think of not singing with Chapel anymore."

Candice nodded and broke off more of the cookie from my hand.

I looked at my phone. "3:08. Time to go," I said.

We walked into the dark music building.

Dr. A was looking over a score and checking his watch when we walked to our places. "Just in time," he said. "Movement five. *Agnus Dei.*"

We flipped through our scores to find the correct section. Candice and I looked at each other in wonder. The entire movement was only three pages long. I scanned the soprano part. Inverted descending scale and then inverted ascending scale. Then the reverse. Three times. That was it. Two months ago just hearing the word "inverted" in relation to a scale would have frightened me, but not any longer. It was still tricky, and I still made mistakes, but our ears were slowly becoming accustomed to sounds that felt wrong but were right.

"This movement is the calm before the storm. *Agnus Dei. Lamb of God.* We need to be quiet here. Our job is to support the tenor. Alright, let's hit it. Here are your starting notes." Dr. A played a chord on the piano, and we found our notes and began.

"*Agnus dei qui tolis peccata mundi,*" we sang. We slipped around on the scales, different people singing different flats and naturals.

Dr. A cut us off. His right hand drew a circle and his fist closed as though catching the end of our note. "Try again," he said, smiling. "You can do this. You have to do this, because the orchestra is coming in at four and we're going to play this together as best we can."

We tried again. "*Agnus dei.*" Lamb of God. I couldn't hear those words without thinking of my grade school years in a small Catholic school. Every Wednesday we walked across the parking lot for mass in the stone church with long pews that were never full except on the night of our Christmas pageant. The church echoed and I sat near the altar with the rest of the choir. There were only ten of us and we did not know how to sing in harmony. "Lamb of God," we sang, "You take away the sins of the world. Have mercy on us." Mrs. Borash, the choir director, told us that when you say your prayers, you pray once, and when you sing them, you pray twice. Singing didn't make me feel so connected to God as it made me feel connected to myself. I felt my air moving through me. I listened to the sound that only I could make.

Dr. A made us stop and start and stop and start. Finally, just before the orchestra came in, we started to make progress. We made our schwas match in tone and pitch, and we added subtle dynamics through crescendos on the ascending scales and decrescendos on the descending scales. By the time the orchestra arrived, we were ready to sing with them. It never went perfectly the first few times we played through new movements with them, but we were always prepared to try.

OWEN AND THE other men in camp train in the mornings and early afternoon. Owen feels himself getting stronger. He must get stronger, for he does not see an end to this war. His only option is to go back and fight, to move forward. Light reflects off the dewy grass and the men walk out of their huts in boots and uniforms, their eyes still heavy from sleep. The commander orders them to run and Owen feels his feet pounding the ground. He puts a hand to his cheek's flush and sheen. A whistle blows and the commander begins to lead them in the game "Do this—Do that." It is an old parlor game, really, but it can be mentally and physically taxing if kept up for a while. The officer shouts, "Do this" and puts an arm straight up in the air. The men imitate his movement. "Do this—" a bending down on one knee. Again, the men follow him. "Do this—" the commander kneels on the other knee. The men do, as well. "Do that—" a jumping up to a standing position. A few men pop up as well, but as soon as they do, they groan and walk off to the sideline. They are out, but Owen is still in. The actions begin to come at a faster pace. Do this, do this, do that, do this. Owen reaches his arms out wide, he balances on one foot, he freezes, he crouches down and places his hands on the grass. Do this, do that, do this, do this. He puts both hands on his head, and he leaves them there and breathes while other men move and are out. He jumps up and down, he bends to touch the tips of his shining boots. More men drop out of the game. Owen begins sweating. The remaining men pant around him. It takes more energy to concentrate than to simply move their bodies in the correct ways. Do this, do that. Owen runs in place like the commander and continues to run when the others stop. He wins the game.

Men come up to him and pat him on the back. No one is upset at having lost. It is a game, and they are all healing. Owen smiles to himself. He feels, for the first time, that he has put his shell shock completely to rest. The commander blows his whistle and the men drop into push-up form. Owen digs his toes into the ground and spreads his fingers wide in the grass. When he pushes his body up, he feels lighter than before. Finally, he can support himself. Finally, he is well.

He continues to do push-up after push-up with ease. Sweat beads at his temples and he forces out his breath with each launch of his body up from the ground. He is better now.

But then his arm muscles give way, and Owen falters. His chest hits the ground. He is better now. He will receive his orders. He will salute, pack his things, and go. He will fight and, maybe, he will die. He breathes in the scent of grass and dirt. Things alive and fresh.

"Owen!" The commander shouts.

He had not noticed that he had stopped moving. With a deep breath and a quick closing, then opening of his eyes, Owen starts again. He pushes his hands on the ground. He spits out air each time he comes up. He keeps going, knowing that the commander's whistle will not blow again for a few minutes, knowing that once it does, he will rest his knees on the ground, take a breath, then stand and wait for whatever comes next. He will obey. He has no choice.

I READ IN a letter from Owen to his mother toward the end of June 1918 that his poems "Hospital Barge" and "Futility" had been published in *The Nation*.

Owen writes that he will send the editor's check to her in early July and that the money can be used to send his brother Colin, a recent cadet in the newly founded Royal Air Force, "into Extravagance." When he tells of his poetry's success, Owen's tone in the letters remains steady, explanatory—not excited, as I would have imagined.

Now, a hundred years later, I feel great joy at reading of his publications. I am especially excited to read that "Futility" has found a place in a magazine. After two years of reading Owen's poems and listening to them in music almost every day, "Futility" has become my favorite. I cannot read the lines, now, without hearing Pears's voice—or, more recently, mine. In the past few months, I have been singing this section of the second movement while washing dishes, packing up my book bags for the library, filling my car with gas. I love the way the words feel in my mouth as I send them out of my body with my breath and with my voice. After listening to Pears sing the poem so many times, I have adopted his inflections and the length of his fermatas. I sing in a different key to fit my range, and I pretend, as I brush my hair before the mirror, as I fill my mug with coffee, as I walk to my car from the library at night, that I am performing the *War Requiem* again, this time as the tenor, sometimes as the baritone. I will still sing the choral parts in order to support the soldier's voices, but I have realized that I sing the Latin parts to myself much less frequently now than I did a year ago. After steeping myself in Owen's world, I understand better, now, why the choral parts are smaller compared to those of the soldiers'.

BRITTEN SITS AT his typewriter. He can hear Pears practicing on the other side of the house, but he trains his mind toward the *Requiem*. The soprano part—though he has not finished writing it yet—will be challenging. The singer must be able to sing with emotion over an enormous choir and orchestra. He cannot settle. He will not.

He writes to the Artistic Director of the Coventry Cathedral Festival that he cannot be sure of the exact specifications of the *Requiem*, but that he knows he would like the choir to be as large as possible. He would like the same for the orchestra. He is planning for triple woodwind and as many as fourteen brass pieces for the *Tuba Mirum* in the second movement. He also tells him that he needs space for the chamber orchestra and that the boys' choir and organ need to be set apart from the rest of the players and instrumentalists. Britten taps his fingers on the typewriter keys without pressing any of them down. It is a lot to ask for, but it must be done. He cannot change the course of the music writing its way in his mind. He closes the letter. "Do write if there are any other queries you want answered. P.S. I still have not decided about the wretched conductor business."

He takes the letter from the typewriter and signs his name. He folds it into an envelope and gets up to bring it to the front hall where he will not forget to grab it on his way to town in the morning. In the other room, Pears sings Schubert. Britten has so much work to do, but he leans against the doorway and watches Pears sing. Pears's eyes flash a smile at him when he sees that Britten has stopped to listen. Pears rests a hand on the piano, beckoning him. Britten smiles and takes his place at the piano. At Pears's next breath, he enters with the accompaniment. Out the window at his back, birds chirp from trees that have begun losing leaves. They make music together. The air around them hums in the oncoming twilight.

I LOOK THROUGH *The Collected Poems of Wilfred Owen*, edited by C. Day Lewis. The first section of this book, labeled "The War Poems" were edited by Seigfried Sassoon and Edith Sitwell shortly after Owen was killed. I watch the stanzas rise and fall as I turn the pages. From "The Last Laugh" I read: "Till, slowly lowered, his whole face kissed the mud. / And the Bayonets' long teeth grinned; / Rabbles of Shells hooted and groaned; / And the Gas hissed." His use of personification brought war's instruments to life. He crammed so many images and so much emotion into his poems, and he still paid close attention to the rhythm and sound housed in each line. But I know that it was not easy for him. Most of his poems went through multiple drafts. I read C. Day Lewis's notes below "Anthem for Doomed Youth" and see that the British Museum has four drafts, Owen's brother Harold has two, and Owen's cousin Leslie Gunston has one. Most of his poems have footnotes to this effect. When I look up his handwritten drafts on the British Museum's website, I see slanted lines with scratches and blots of ink. Cramped words float above excisions. The poems look labored over.

I close the collection and hold it in both hands. I look down at the photograph of Owen in his officer's uniform on the cover. His shoulders stoop just the tiniest bit forward. His hands fold in front of him, his wrists and forearms piped in gold with diamond-shaped buttons lining the cuffs. A leather strap crosses his chest and connects to a holster against his left hip. His eyes are sad.

BRITTEN READS OWEN'S poetry again and again, waiting for melodies to strike him. Often they come easily. Owen's lines have rhymes that don't quite lock into one another—"sun" and "unsown," "once" and "France," "star and stir." Britten likes this about them. When he reads the words aloud, some of the sounds barrel out of him, harsh and hard, while others flow softly from his lips like breath. Who was this man who wrote these words—"The shrill, demented choirs of wailing shells"—these words that are now slowly becoming a part of Britten himself? He whispers them while he rinses out his empty cup of tea. "Not in the hands of boys, but in their eyes / Shall shine the holy glimmers of goodbyes." He whistles the tunes that he thinks will support the poetry while he goes on walks around the Red House. "And each slow dusk a drawing-down of blinds." Sometimes he stands beside the old maple that somehow rises both humble and triumphant outside his studio window and sings some of the sections that course through his head all day and night, an unrelenting and strange, strange river.

Often, though, he suffers doubt. How can he—one man—hope to live up to the strength of the Requiem Mass and the deep truth and poignancy of Owen's poems? Britten fears that he is Icarus, flying too close to the sun.

Britten takes a break from writing and walks out into the yard. He leans against the maple's trunk and looks up at the leaves shivering in the wind. A few break from their branches and flutter down to his feet. Britten sings a melodic idea for "Futility," the poem that Pears will sing in the quiet middle of the *Dies Irae*:

Move him into the sun—
Gently its touch awoke him once,
At home, whispering of fields half-sown.
Always it woke him, even in France,
Until this morning and this snow.
If anything might rouse him now
The kind old sun will know.

What did Owen look like? Britten can picture a young face, a kind face. Deep eyes of a dark brown. Yet his imagination fails him. He wants to see him. He wants to see the face that saw the horrors of war, took those horrors inside of himself, and created this poetry.

The wind picks up and more November leaves fall down around him. Britten walks out from under the maple and looks at the dark storm clouds rolling in from the west. He stands still, arms at his sides, face lifted to the sky, until he feels the first drops of rain on his cheeks and hands. Then he stands a bit longer and breathes in the scent of earth becoming wet. He imagines the young poet standing in a muddy trench, the rain soaking through his clothes and dampening the half-written poems tucked in his coat pocket. He can envision Owen's pale hands reaching inside his coat to cover the paper from the rain. He wishes he could see in person the face of the man who died too young and too soon, whose body was pocked by bullets near a river in France and was buried there.

The cold rain finds the lines in Britten's face and streams down them like tears. He imagines the same happening to Owen: rain finding worry—no, terror—lines in a face that had been young not long ago, a face made old by war.

Britten opens his eyes to the sky and does not know if he is crying or if the water falling from his eyes is just rain. He walks inside, and, with hands that feel waterlogged, cold, and stiff, he puts on the kettle. He waits to grow warm.

I TRAVEL FROM Virginia to Minnesota for two weeks in early spring of 2015, and while I'm there, I read a little and I write even less, and I spend hours just driving around Minneapolis. I do not know how the neighborhoods connect and looking at maps doesn't help me. Instead, I drive from Northeast to Longfellow to Hiawatha to Nokomis and try to figure out how my city is pieced together. As I drive, I think about the *War Requiem* and the lives that I am weaving together on paper. I am drawing my own map of strange constellations made from letters, recordings, biographies and—strangest of all—my own thoughts and feelings and questions that have surprised me with their intensity from the moment I began rehearsing the *War Requiem* two years ago.

For the first time, I miss my house in Virginia. I miss the pictures on the walls, the scraps of notes written in excited haste while I listened to the music, the stacks of biographies whose pages I've flipped so many times. I step out of the car and shut the door and stare up the street where I have lived for most of my life and notice that I feel a little bit lost. I have made a home in the *War Requiem*.

Later, before I leave to go back to Virginia, I meet my cousin, Anna, at the restaurant we always go to, a tiny barbecue place inside a converted garage. In the summertime, the glass garage windows roll up and the tables get scooted out to the garden area, where twinkle lights hang above small trees and yellow umbrellas. This evening, though, a cold wind blows beneath the gray sky and we huddle inside among the other diners. Anna is my senior by two years. Growing up, we put on performances for our family; she played the piano and I sang. It always amazed me how easily she could sight read the Disney medleys I asked her to play. I usually sang a breathy "Think of Me" from *Phantom of the Opera* as a warm-up act to her flawless, fingers-flying Mozart concertina that she could bang out from memory as a thirteen-year-old. I was in awe of Anna.

We have not seen each other in months and we meet on this night to celebrate the fact that Anna would soon leave Minnesota to study T.S. Eliot for her Ph.D. in English. She tells me that a professor explained to her that in order to fully understand Modernism and the era in which T.S. Eliot wrote, she must study the writing that came out of World War I. When I tell Anna about my fascination with Wilfred Owen, she leans in close over her beer and dish of yucca fries. "It's so interesting that both of us are drawn to the same time period," she says.

I feel woefully ashamed that I did not know for certain even as little as the dates and countries involved in the war until the *War Requiem* led me there. The *War Requiem* has brought me to so many places. Never before have I thought about my life and its position in time with so much attention and so much emotion. The grandfather Anna and I share, a musician and conductor, fought in World War II when he was twenty-seven years old. He was born in 1914, the year World War I began. My grandfather's life overlapped Wilfred Owen's by only four years, yet it feels like another link to me. The space and time between us collapse a bit more.

6. LIBERA ME

"In paradisum deducant te Angeli..."

"Into Paradise may the angels lead thee..."

WIND PUMMELED THICK raindrops against the windows, but soon our hundred voices drowned out the world beyond the glass. It was March 2013, and I tilted my head from side to side while humming scales and massaging the back of my neck. Dr. A held up his score and we opened our own to the *Libera Me*. I felt nervous about this last movement; it was over twenty pages and featured a fugue made of sixteenth notes that spanned two octaves. Before learning the *War Requiem*, I hadn't known what a fugue was, but had since learned it was a counterpoint composition where a melody is introduced by one part and then taken up by the others to form music that sounds interwoven. Now, I would be learning a complex fugue and performing it within a month.

When I paged through the sixth movement, the notes I saw looked frantic. Double barred sixteenth notes sprawled thirds and fourths on the staff. Time signatures switched from two-four to two-two to four-five and back to two-four on a single page. Worst of all, if the choral part looked this difficult, that meant that the orchestra would be playing something so challenging as to be insane; we would not be able to depend on the instrumentalists to help us along in our singing. We would be on our own. Sometimes I felt ready to look at Dr. A and shake my head, ask him: How do you believe we can do this? We were not professional musicians. We were college kids. Most of us were English or biology majors.

After we warmed up, Dr. A sent each vocal part to a separate rehearsal room. We would learn the fugue on our own as sopranos and become solid in the part as a section before trying it with the full chorus. Candice and I followed our section leader, a music major named Katherine, to a small rehearsal room above our Chapel Choir space. The room had many white shutters blocking out skinny windows on the far side. We walked toward the grand piano in the corner and clustered together in our approximate order. Katherine gave us our note. "This is really high, so let's sing an octave below on *ta*."

She counted us off slowly and we took a deep breath. "*Ta-a, ta, ta, ta, ta, ta.*" As we sang, we slipped away from each other melodically.

Katherine held up a hand to stop us and played a fresh note. "Let's start again. Let's go slower."

We sang the four measures that contained the fugue over and over, slowly gaining speed and accuracy, but still, it was nowhere near where it needed to be for performance. When the fugue was played up to tempo, the sopranos sang over seventy notes within forty seconds. After singing through the fugue on *ta* about ten times slower than it would be sung in performance, we realized that it would be easiest to sing if memorized. Though the score held all of the answers, sometimes it was impossible to follow along at the speed required to sing accurately.

After practicing with the sopranos alone for thirty minutes, we picked up our scores and joined the rest of the choir. Dr. A played our notes. "Sopranos," he called out. Our voice part led the fugue, with the other parts entering and complicating the melody sometimes just a quarter rest behind us. He played our starting note again and we planted our feet and took a deep breath. He counted us in and we sang the first note, then the second note, and then we fell apart and ended in strangled-sounding sighs. I felt embarrassed. We messed up in front of the whole choir after thirty minutes of diligent practice.

But then Dr. A smiled at us, told us not to worry but to try again, and I felt myself fall back into the space of trust that we had been cultivating together for the past three years in Chapel Choir. He believed in us so fervently that it was difficult not to believe in ourselves.

We started again and we warred against the music, slapped the scores to our foreheads, looked at our neighbors and laughed. How could we sing this music? How could something so hard and strange even exist? Every day in choir was a constant back and forth between despair and an almost excruciating high when we managed to get something—no matter how small—right. We were fighting for that little bit of right. Dr. A held his arms open to us and we followed the movement of his wrists. We would try again. We would keep trying.

BRITTEN FINALLY HEARS Galina Vishnevskaya sing in person about a year before the *War Requiem* is to premiere. She and Rostropovich have come to London, and Vishnevskaya is set to give a performance which Britten and Pears attend.

In the audience, Britten wrings the program between his hands. Depending on how this performance goes, Britten will either have his soprano, or he will be back in the search. So often the voice unlocks the melodies for him. It is so much easier, for instance, to write for Pears than to write a straight tenor line. When he can hear the technique and color of the voice, he knows exactly what he can put on the page. He knows how much he can push it, how much he can demand, and how much freedom he can leave for interpretation by the musician.

The lights dim in the house and Britten puts a hand on Pears's own. Vishnevskaya walks on to applause along with the conductor. Vishnevskaya, with her black pompadour and her outlined eyes, appears both intense and sophisticated. The conductor holds up his baton, and with a quick flick back and forth the orchestra begins playing. Vishnevskaya stands tall and statuesque; she barely moves as she takes a breath before her entrance.

The minute Britten hears her voice ringing out, he knows it is the one that matches the soprano melodies that have been quietly spinning themselves in his mind. The sound is full and round—even more so than on her recordings—and she has complete control of her instrument. The vibrato is even, consistent. Britten closes his eyes and lets her tone flow over him. Somehow she manages to sing both forcefully and gently within the span of two notes.

When she finishes singing, Britten applauds and stands. Afterward, when he and Pears meet Rostropovich and Vishnevskaya outside of the theater, he tells her of his composition and asks for her participation. He worries that the little English she knows will not be enough to understand what he asks of her, but she gives him one of her dazzling smiles and nods. Then she reaches out her arms and embraces him.

THE DAY FEELS heavy to Owen. He stands in the doorway of the hut in Ripon and folds his arms about himself against the chill. He closes his eyes as a gust of wind blows small needles of rain to his face. When the wind quiets, he opens his eyes and looks to the horizon. Grayness clings to the landscape. He can see mist in the distance; it's raining in those far-off places, places he can't reach. He wonders if rain is falling on his childhood home in Shrewsbury.

Today must be near the anniversary of his shell shock's onset. Has it only been a year? It seems a lifetime of heaviness has been filling all the spaces in his body. Sometimes, when he is busy running drills or walking into town beneath a glowing sun, he feels almost normal, almost the way he did before entering the war. Usually, though, he feels the burden of death settling in his veins like mud. This feeling, he knows, he will carry until his last breath. How many men has he seen dead? Too many to count. Almost too many to continue on with the business of being alive in a world where lives can be extinguished with such ease.

Another gust of wind blows into Owen, but he does not turn his back against the rain. These pinpricks of water, these little bits of pain—these cannot harm him. Owen wishes that he could go inside and sit by the fire with his dear friend, Sassoon. He has not heard from him in a while, and he misses him. Sassoon understood and could articulate those dark and chaotic sensations that coursed through Owen's thoughts. When Owen told him of the premonition he had always had when young—that he was going to die, and soon—Sassoon just shook his head and rested a hand on his shoulder. Those small gestures were enough to calm Owen and assuage his fears.

He wraps his arms around himself tighter. He misses his friend.

He misses his life. He can put his breath into the line, put his hopelessness into words, but he cannot feel that hand on his shoulder, cannot hear his mother's voice. He is separate and alone. He is lonely, so lonely.

I SLOWLY REALIZE that when I move away from Virginia after graduating, I will lose access to the collections of letters. Finding them in libraries is difficult, and besides, I want to own them. I want these books for myself. I begin researching places to buy the books online and despair falls over me. The most inexpensive copy of the *Collected Letters* I can find is $122.65, and the books are broken into three parts. One full copy tops out at $728.21. These prices do not cover the cost to ship the collections from England. I see a picture online of the same green book that sits at my table now. It comes from Germany and costs $145 plus $10 for shipping. I want the book so badly that I feel my heart rate tick up a notch. I begin searching the Minnesota library system and find collected letters of just about everyone, but not of Wilfred Owen. Suddenly, the fact that I have come by these books so easily seems a sort of magic. I turn the pages carefully. I feel their measured weight.

OWEN WRITES TO his mother asking for a dozen bars of soap. He needs razors, too, but he doesn't want to ask for too much at once. Owen runs his hands through his hair and feels the coarseness that comes with sweat and mud and little access to soap and water. This is a small discomfort, he knows, but still, tonight he wants nothing more than to slip into a warm bath and lie there, submerged and safe.

I READ A letter that Britten writes to German conductor Otto Klemperer. In it, he says, "My great aim as a composer is to find exactly the right notes to say what I have to say—down to the last [drawing of a sixteenth note]! I cannot, alas, pretend I always succeed, as all my best loved composers do, but I try and try."

When I think of how confused I was in rehearsals for the *War Requiem*, I shake my head in wonder at Britten. How did he *know*? How did he know that all those crazy, dissonant, terrible notes were right? Not just right, but *precisely* right? I feel as though I could fit each note in the *War Requiem* on the head of a pin and it would balance, perfect and round and sure. It is we—the musicians, the singers—who make it difficult with our imperfections in technique, tone, and blend. The notes themselves are ready and waiting for whomsoever can attack them with the right amounts of ferocity, precision, and tact.

I feel similarly when I read Owen's drafts and poems. He pored over each word, positive that these poems were the correct vessels for his thoughts. He trusted them to carry his voice beyond his death and into the future.

I know that both Britten and Owen struggled with their creations. I see it in the way Owen crossed out words with thick double-lines, wrote new ones beside them only to strike them again. I see it in the letters I read of Britten's where he discussed illness after illness as he labored over his music. And I know that I have had difficulties while writing this book. Some sections have flown out from under my typing fingertips so quickly it is as though I weren't writing at all, but only breathing, being. Other times I have typed and deleted and typed and deleted a single word over and over, a monotonous drone of deafening insecurity trapping me along with that one word fighting its way to the page. I have written hundreds of pages that I have printed out, pored over, and ultimately cut. I have put this manuscript away for months at a time, convinced that maybe this book was only meant to be written and read by me and not read by others. I have doubted my ability to create and I have doubted my worth as an artist even as the sentences have spilled out of me, even as I sensed small sparks lighting the way along my lines, urging me that, yes, they hold truth—yes, they hold beauty—yes, they deserve to exist.

I think of Owen's and Britten's precision within their groundbreaking works, and I wonder: How does an artist know what is right? How does an artist know how to translate the alchemy that occurs among the silvery wisps of the mind, the beating heat of the chest, the minute flickerings of wind against skin, sound of pond peepers in the dark, sight of bright and fluttering leaves before one's eyes? How do we put all that we think and feel on a page or canvas or in the trill of a flute or in the snap of a camera shutter? How do we do all of that? How do we contain it in a form that can be revisited and pondered over?

I am neither poet nor composer, but in writing this book, I have had to become both.

Britten died after a celebrated career and Owen died without knowing how famous he would become. Neither one of them would ever have considered that their spheres of influence would reach an American woman in her twenties and that she would learn everything she could about them. That she would imagine them so fiercely that they became her friends. And that small miracle, lonely miracle—my friendship with these men I've never met—makes me sit at my kitchen table with my head resting in my palm, quiet memories of things I've never seen spiraling out before me like magic I'm not afraid to borrow any longer.

In January of 1962, Britten and Pears rent a place in Greece where Britten will work on the Coventry Commission. Their rental is small, but there is a piano and a desk and wide windows that frame gulls swooping over the vivid Aegean Sea.

Britten turns to the libretto where he has sketched out the second movement. Something in one of the tenor's lines during the setting of "Anthem for Doomed Youth" catches his attention each time he runs through it in his mind. He calls for Pears who is reading in the other room. "Peter, will you come sing this for me?" He listens to the quiet thunk of a book closing. "Are you warmed up enough?" Pears practiced earlier in the day, but it has been a few hours.

Pears nods and hums a few quick scales and Britten feels that small bloom of gratitude in his chest at hearing Pears's voice preparing to sing for him—only for him and to help him.

"Sing gently. There's something about the words. The melody is fine, I think." Britten moves to the piano and Pears takes a seat beside him on the bench. "Here, these lines here." Britten plays through the melody quickly and Pears sings softly under his breath. "Got them?"

Pears nods. Britten moves his right hand back and forth and counts him in. He plays a mixture of the melody and the short chords that the strings will play in counterpoint.

Pears sings, "The pallor of girls' brows shall be their pall; / Their flowers the tenderness of patient minds, / And each slow dusk a drawing-down of blinds."

Britten lifts his hands off the keys. "There, it's there in that penultimate line. Something is sticking." He reaches for the Owen poetry collection and thumbs through the pages until he finds "Anthem for Doomed Youth."

Pears stands. "I'm going to grab some water. I'll be right back."

Britten waves him off with an "All right, all right," as he re-reads the poem and the footnotes provided by the editor C. Day Lewis. The second footnote addresses the line that gives him trouble:

> BM [The British Museum] has alternatives, *silent* and *patient*, together with a deleted variant, *sweet white*…Owen did not hit upon *silent* till the final draft: patient was then penciled in, presumably at SS's [Seigfried Sassoon's] suggestion when Owen showed him the poem at Craiglockhart in September, 1917.

"Peter, come here," Britten calls. In the libretto he writes "sweet white" and "silent" above the word "patient."

"I'm coming, I'm coming," Pears says. He emerges, a glass of water in hand. He takes his place and leans over to set the glass down on the nearby table.

"All right, try singing this line with 'sweet white' instead of 'patient.'"

Britten furrows his brow and closes his eyes when Pears sings "Their flowers the tenderness of sweet white minds."

He lifts his hands off the keys. "No, the words sound too swift within the rhythm. The vowels don't match up and the *t*'s sound too harsh. This moment should be quieter to go along with the ascending scale, don't you think? You sound lovely, by the way. Try it with 'silent.'"

Britten counts them in and Pears sings again, this time: "Their flowers the tenderness of silent minds."

"That's it, that's it," Britten says. "That fits much better. Thank you, dear." Britten crosses out "patient" and "sweet white," leaving "silent," content that it was the word that Owen selected in the end, too.

Hands that were just like his own had built these walls—hands that had measured and mortared over a thousand years ago. Owen decided to walk to the Aldborough ruins this morning despite the overcast sky that appeared like a milky film over his vision when he opened his eyes at dawn. Now, walking around stone walls that come up to his knees, he feels confident that the sun's rays will pierce through the dense sky. He breathes in the country air around him, his hands resting on his chest. He stands still and looks down to the backs of his hands that rise with each blooming breath. He looks about him, at the past that so clearly remains in the midst of the present. He walks down the narrow pathway toward the great flat squares of mosaics, still with his hands rising and falling on his chest. This art has lasted for centuries in rain, wind, snow, and sun. The ceramic black has faded to charcoal, but it is still here. People have always needed to create, to have their creations witnessed by someone else. He kneels down to the mosaic and places his hands on the tiles. Grays and light browns and creamy whites braid together and fold in on each other until they meet at an eight-pointed star in the center, and in the center of that: a perfect circle. Romans created this mosaic when they came into Britain in the fourth century.

Owen remains crouched by the mosaic, his hands flat on the cool tile. He picks his head up toward the breeze.

He will receive word soon that he has made it into the next Division. After that, only one more will remain before he is sent back into battle.

I have not opened the *Collected Letters of Wilfred Owen* for a few weeks now. I have not wanted to because I know that the end is near. Finally,

I open the yellowed pages to April of 1918, seven months before he will die. Owen is still in Ripon, still in training, still writing letters to his mother every few days. I read through ten letters quickly and suddenly find myself halfway through May. I force myself to go back and read the letters again. I add to my notes, circling sections that I want to write about with a green marker.

Time is moving too fast for me.

Over the course of April, Owen's letters reference his Division placement in the training camp many times. At first he is in Division Four, and this lulls me into thinking that I have more time with him; he has a while yet before he will be placed in Division One and sent back to the front. But then, just a few letters later, he writes to his mother that he has now made it to Division Three. I feel my chest tighten. Don't get well, I want to whisper to the pages. Fake a relapse, I wish I could say. But I know that he wouldn't, and didn't. I know that nobody would fake shell shock, not after actually experiencing it or witnessing the tremors and shouts of those broken by war. Owen doesn't fight for glory. A different virtue blooms inside him as it does in the hearts of his fellow soldiers: truth. They will not let their truths be broken by this cruel war.

I wonder what Susan Owen's reactions were to these letters, his notice to her that he had moved up a level. Of course she would want her son to get better. Of course she would want the terrible dreams and the burden of living so closely with death lifted from his shoulders, evaporated. But she had to have feared that his healing would be his downfall.

BRIGHT SUNLIGHT SHINES through the hut's window this morning upon the men's waking. Owen rolls onto his back, stretches his arms above his head and lies still for a moment. He pretends that he is back in his childhood home and that Harold and Colin sleep nearby. Downstairs, his mother makes tea and toast. Owen remembers coming upon her in the kitchen, her head haloed by the sun's light, their eyes and hands meeting as she passed him a cup of hot tea. His days were open and full of promise, then.

The men around him get dressed and squat on the edges of their cots, lacing their boots. Owen rests with his eyes toward the glowing window for one more moment before stirring himself from bed. He dresses slowly, taking care with each button and tucking his shirt in smoothly. When he bends to tie his boots, he rubs off a clump of dirt with the back of a loose fist. The men have started leaving the hut for this morning's lecture and Owen follows at a distance. He breathes in the morning air and watches the sun glisten on their hair. They walk quickly. Owen steps into their dewy footprints left behind in the grass. It is as though they are all children going off for an adventure together. If only they could walk past the building where the lecture will take place and keep walking. They could walk clear to the edge of England and start wading into the blue. They would take off their uniforms and let them sink in the water. They would float together across oceans.

The men have all disappeared into the building, and Owen picks up his pace. He slips into the room and finds a place to sit just as the speaker, a Captain from the War Office, takes his place behind the podium. He looks out over the men with a stern face and clears his throat before speaking. Owen listens to his voice, loud and straight-edged as a bayonet. The Captain tells them that he has heard great things about their training and that he believes that soon all of them will be back where they belong: fighting. Even if they are not currently at the front, they are still doing everything they can for their country and that is commendable and appreciated by everyone in Britain.

The Captain tells them that the Germans are still putting forth a good fight, and that the Allies need all of the men still in training to keep working hard and moving ahead in Divisions in order to get back on the field and kill as many Huns as they can. Owen can sense the men around him tense with excitement and purpose. They react to this speech the way they are supposed to. They are being made to see that their use in this life is to give their life to war.

Owen clutches his hands together and tries to preserve a pocket of air inside them. In this pocket he holds his vision of himself and all the other soldiers floating together in pale blue water. He squeezes his fingers together tightly around the vision in his hands. He will not let it be tarnished by the Captain's words. He closes his eyes against the thunderous roar of applause as the Captain bows on stage. He imagines himself drifting, drifting, far away.

After the lecture, Owen walks back to the hut, anger filling him with each step. Inside, he pulls out his poetry with so much force that papers fly from the folder. He scoops them up and finds an envelope addressed to him. He scrounges around his belongings and pushes aside socks, his mess tin, knife, and blanket to find a pen. He sits on the edge of his cot, envelope flipped so his address presses against his thigh. Seething, he reminds himself to breathe.

> Head to limp head, sunk-eyed wounded scanned
> Yesterday's news; the casualties (typed small)
> And (large) Vast Booty from our Latest Haul.

Listening to the Captain, it was clear what his priorities were and were not. They were not the soldiers sitting before him or the millions of civilians whose lives had ended and would continue to end because of this war. All the Captain cared about was winning and preserving his own power and prestige.

> Peace would do wrong to our undying dead,
> Our glorious sons might even regret they died
> If we got nothing lasting in their stead.

He scrawled the rest of the draft across the back of the envelope, each line thick and sneering. Then the title across the top: "Smile, smile, smile."

TODAY I READ a letter Britten wrote to the Coventry Cathedral music director, Alec Robertson, who wrote the program note for the premiere of the *War Requiem* during the Coventry Festival. Britten writes about the *Requiem*: "I was completely absorbed in this piece, as really never before—but with considerable agony in finding the adequate notes for such a subject (& such words!) & dread discovering that I've not succeeded. Whether it will work or not I can't say, but I had to say & do it."

This is how I feel, writing about Britten and Owen and this piece of music that joins their lives together and that joins their lives to mine. *Whether it will work or not I can't say, but I had to say & do it.*

OWEN GOES TO London in May of 1918 and sleeps three hours total over the course of two days and nights. All of these hours awake are spent in restaurants and cafés with editors and writers. Due to the dwindling paper supply, a book of his poems will not be able to come out until next spring, but Owen can hardly think about that. It all seems unreal; it has all happened so fast, and so much of it when he was in the trenches, in the hospital, the hotel, and now in the huts of Ripon. He has had only a few poems published, and the fact that people are buzzing about him in restaurants, shaking his hand, and talking about a forthcoming book, is unbelievable.

I HAVE BEEN reading letters and though it is late, I am hungry, and I search the cupboards in my cottage's kitchen for something to eat. I find a bag of rice and a few granola bars; it's been a while since I've gone to the grocery store. I set the *Collected Letters* on my kitchen table and set a pot of water on the stove, placing its lid on top. I sit down at my kitchen table and push aside the printed sheets of my writing, the *Requiem* score, the scribbled notes on Post-its that have unstuck themselves from my walls. I open the book and when I turn the pages to my place, I feel that same moment of panic that, lately, has taken hold of me each time I read Owen's letters. Every letter I read, I come closer to the end. I have less than forty pages left.

I focus on the letter's date and try to ignore the sharp pain that has wedged itself in my chest. May 25, 1918. Owen writes to his mother about the latest poem he is working on. He calls it "The Deranged," but I learn from the footnote that this poem becomes "Mental Cases." In the letter, Owen has written that the editor of the *Burlington Magazine*, William More Adey, has "solemnly prohibited" him from sending the poem to the *English Review*. Owen tells his mother that his head does not spin from words like this as it would have five years ago. It is exciting, of course, but fame and acclaim are not his end goals. He writes:

> I am old already for a poet, and so little is yet achieved.
> And I want no limelight, and celebrity is the last infirmity I desire. <u>Fame is the recognition of one's peers.</u>
> I have already more than their recognition: I have the silent and immortal friendship of Graves and Sassoon and those. Behold are they not already as many Keatses?

I realize that I am reading aloud as if I were reading a poem. His short paragraphs lend themselves to becoming poetic lines. I continue. I let my voice grow stronger:

> As I looked out into the untraveled world over the hedges of Dunsden Garden, I saw them in the dawn and made ready to go out and meet them.
> And they were glad and rejoiced, though I am the gravest and least witty of that grave, witty company.
> Today I climbed back over the hedges into Dunsden again and wandered round the parish for hours. (For this ordinary

There the letter stops and the editors have inserted a note that the remainder is missing. I wonder how the last part of this letter was lost— did a page blow away from Susan Owen's hand as she read the letter, walking back from the post? Was the letter shared with Harold, and did he, then, somehow misplace it? Perhaps Susan Owen decided to keep the next part for herself. There is no way for me to know. I can only be grateful for the words I have.

I go back and read the letter again out loud. At first, the end of the letter conjures in my mind images of Owen reaching his friends in some heavenly place. Then I remember that Owen lived in the Dunsden vicarage from 1911 to 1913. When writing this letter, Owen is imagining himself back before he entered the war, back before his poetry led him to Graves and Sassoon. He was looking to the future from the past. "As I looked out into the untraveled world over the hedges of Dunsden Garden, I saw them in the dawn and made ready to go out and meet them," he wrote. *I saw them in the dawn.* Owen describes himself as so grateful for these friendships to be—so grateful, that he could only express himself in poetry.

I read the line again and then close my eyes. I picture Owen leaning out a window at the Dunsden vicarage, seeing the outlines of his close friends standing in pale light. In my mind, I watch him exit the house and climb over the hedges, walking, then running to join them. I do not picture them meeting over the rails of hospital beds. I do not picture them comforting one another while the other shakes and screams and cannot wake from dreams of death. I picture them as Owen does, happy and free, standing in the light.

AFTER A MONTH in Greece—traveling to Mycenae, Argos, Olympia, Tiryns, Epidaurus, Delphi, Asini—Britten and Pears arrive back home at the Red House in Aldeburgh. He has finished writing the Coventry commission. He walks into his studio and sets his briefcase on the round table, unzips it, and takes out the finished score, not yet bound. He moves books out of the way and drops the briefcase to the floor. He places the score on the table and puts his hands on either side of it. It feels right to have this work back in his studio—so much of it originated here. Owen's lines found their melodies at this table, from the armchair by the window, beneath the grand old tree in the yard. Britten opens the score and slowly turns the pages. He looks at the notes, the sharps and naturals, the flats and time signatures. It will be hard to coax the correct notes out of the orchestra and choir. But he has made it this far, and he will see the piece through to the end. Britten puts the pages together and picks up the score. He holds the sheet music to his chest. The *War Requiem.*

He was five years old when Owen died at twenty-five. If he had survived the war, Owen would be sixty-nine years old at this moment. He would have books upon books of poems published. Perhaps this project could have been a collaboration. Britten closes his eyes and imagines sitting at a table with Owen. Both of them bend over music and poems whose lines can shift and change by the hands of their creators. He sees the two of them together, smiling in lamplight, drinking cups of tea that cooled hours ago. One old man, and the other growing old, both using their writing to stand together against war.

Britten opens his eyes. He wants to throw the score across the room, watch the pages spread like snow. Tonight, Britten came home. Owen never got to. Tonight, he brought home a piece of music that he was able to finish. He was able to languish in the sun, feel its heat, and write until he grew tired. He didn't have to squat in a wet trench and write with a dull pencil. He didn't have to write between dreams that threatened to tear him from his sanity. He didn't have to run from shells or bullets or bayonets. He didn't have to worry that at any moment he might meet death.

Britten's hands shake at his sides. He sits down at the desk and takes a pen in his quaking hand. Beneath the title, he crosses out his previous dedication that read: "In Commemoration of all the Fellow-Sufferers of the Second World War."

He has not suffered.

He pauses, then he writes: "My subject is War, and the pity of War. The Poetry is in the pity. All a poet can do is to warn. —Wilfred Owen" He sits back in his chair and stares at the lines until they blur.

I HEAR THE crackle and hiss of water hitting flame. The water has boiled over. I dump rice in the pot and return to my kitchen table where I balance my laptop on a pile of paper and search for the poem "Mental Cases" online. The minute I finish reading, I remember the letter where Owen writes that he values the esteem of his friends and fellow poets more than fame and I understand why. Part of the poem reads:

These are men whose minds the Dead have ravished...
Always they must see these things and hear them,
Batter of guns and shatter of flying muscles,
Carnage incomparable, and human squander
Rucked too thick for these men's extrication.

Therefore still their eyeballs shrink tormented
Back into their brains, because on their sense
Sunlight seems a blood-smear; night comes blood-black;
Dawn breaks open like a wound that bleeds afresh...

Now, after the reading the poem, the dawn he wrote about in the letter about his friends has shifted in my imagining of Owen's life. In my mind, the sky fades from pale yellow to gray. After his time in war, dawn would never be the same. Even something as innocent as morning light had been marred by the atrocities of war.

I try to imagine the way Owen would have worked over these lines again and again—they are too precise not to have been wrought carefully. I can picture him writing in quick bursts and then pulling the paper out from his coat pocket, reading the words quietly but forcefully out loud, feeling the shape of the words in his mouth, and crossing out and adding in and crossing out again. The way he portrays the gruesome reality of the battlefield and the waste of life was groundbreaking in his time. Up until this point, though some war poetry was graphic, most would have espoused the ideals of honorable sacrifice, heroism, and duty. Owen's poems did not do that. If they were to talk about heroism or duty, it would have been done through irony. If they were to talk about sacrifice, it would not have been about sacrificing one's life for a greater cause, but sacrificing the very real and worthwhile lives that soldiers had lived up until the moment of their death.

In "Mental Cases," Owen repeats the word "blood" again and again, drawing the reader back to the undeniable fact that these soldiers were living people—they were not Romantic ideals of men serving their country, they were not extended metaphors to be used to glorify a government on a plot of land, they were not mere pawns to be placed in service of their superiors. They were people. People full of blood and flesh, people "treading blood from lungs that had loved laughter." People whose "eyeballs shrink tormented / back into their brains." Owen took Sassoon's advice to sweat his guts out writing poetry. He smeared the guts of all those fallen soldiers on the page. He refused to perform his duty silently and let his voice—his beliefs about what war truly made of people—fall away from him unwritten and unsaid, ghostly.

At the level of syntax and diction, the poem astounds me. Sometimes on the first read, the lines feel effortless. But then I find myself whispering the lines out loud at my kitchen table. The attention to sound and to the placement of those sounds is so minute, so precise. Take the line, "carnage incomparable, and human squander." The repeated "ah" sounds in "carnage," "incomparable," and "squander," force the mouth to grow tall and open. I say the words to myself and feel as though I'm crying out in pain. The open vowel sounds make me read slowly, but then I get a short reprieve with the syntactical quick-step of "and human" before I must slow down once again. I cannot escape the pain, the slow agony of the violent, brutal physicality of war. The carnage. The squander. Owen forces the reader to sit with that which is not only uncomfortable but unbearable.

Every line is like this. Every line teeters between anger and despair. But he is not helpless. He is never helpless, though he might be hopeless. He wrote down the horrors of war so that people who had never seen war would be forced to reckon with them. He also provided a mirror for those who had: You are not alone, he wrote. I am witnessing this, as you are. I bear witness to all that you have seen and felt.

DURING THE LAST few days of May in 1918, Owen spends time outside whenever he has a break from training. The German Air Force had launched a raid on London in recent weeks, killing many civilians. At the end of April, three British divisions held off thirteen German divisions at the Battle of Lys. Recently, the Germans attacked French troops along the Aisne River, but the French kept their hold thanks to reinforcements from the United States. All around Europe blood spills, but today Owen floats on his back in the river. The sun glints between the leaves above him and he stretches out his arms on either side of his body. The cool water laps against his skin. Around him, other men splash and laugh and swim. If Owen keeps staring up at the sun, he can imagine that they are all boys, playing and carefree. It is when he stands in the river and looks about him that he sees the scarred bodies, the clouded eyes of his fellow injured men. So, he does not stand. He floats. He feels the sun dance across his face.

Overall, life here in Ripon has been good. Yesterday, he and a friend played a game of tennis during their afternoon off. At one point, when they took a break to switch court sides, Owen turned his back on the camp and looked out across Yorkshire's land. Yellow and purple flowers lit up the fields like sunshine from below. His heart still pounded from the match, his brow was slick with sweat. He had breathed in sweet air and held his palms out to the sun in thanks. The world was still beautiful and he was living in it.

TONIGHT A STORM breaks over the Roanoke Valley, where I live. Rain pelts down on the roof of my cottage and I feel the thunder's vibrations rumbling beneath my feet. I pour myself a glass of wine and sit at the desk chair I have rolled into the kitchen. I look up at the photos of Britten and Owen on my walls, and I read an excerpt from a letter that Britten's teacher, Frank Bridge, wrote to him, that I have taped to the wall beneath the pictures: "We are all 'revelations' as you know. Just go on expanding." Tonight I feel closer to understanding what that means. I have thought about or sung part of the *Requiem* every day for the past two and a half years. I have built a world—a small world, a world that only I know—but a world around the three of us: Britten, Owen, and me. This world—stretching across time and place, music and poetry—is both outside of and within me. It feels cosmic in scope at the same time that it feels hallowed and intimate, resting somewhere deep inside my chest. It is a space I retreat to and a space I explore. I could never have guessed that a piece of music could become so much.

I sit with my knees pulled up to my chest, my head tilted toward the faces of Britten and Owen captured in small moments in time. The storm rolls over my house and then away into the distance. I close my eyes, and still I see their faces. I know them without knowing them. I go on expanding.

AT ST. OLAF, the orchestra filed into our rehearsal room with their instruments. We stretched our arms above our heads and took sips from our water bottles while the instrumentalists set their scores on their music stands and scraped their chairs across the floor, searching for the correct distance from score and neighbor. I watched them tune their instruments and make small jokes with each other over their shoulders. I wondered if they were nervous; I certainly was. We were going to sing the sixth movement with them for the first time and I still didn't think I knew all of my notes. Dr. A had told us to practice on our own, but when I had opened the score in a practice room and sat down at the piano to plunk out the notes, I grew overwhelmed and struggled to find even the first few musical phrases.

Dr. A was talking and laughing with the orchestra director. I didn't understand how he could be laughing when his choir was surely about to melodically crash into the orchestra's playing. We had less than a month until our premiere, and all I could see ahead of us was failure. I felt nervous. My stomach tightened. I turned to Candice, who was humming while following the notes on the score along with her finger. "Can I listen to you?" I whispered. She nodded and held her score open toward me. I leaned in and listened to her, and after a minute I oriented myself in her tiny slice of the music, and I joined in with my own, quiet hum.

The First Violin stood and played an A. The orchestra began tuning together, and we fell silent, waiting. When they finished, Dr. A took his place on the stand. He didn't open his giant score. His music wasn't there at all. It was behind him, resting on a lone music stand. I leaned in toward Candice. "Is he off-book?" I whispered. She looked at me wide-eyed and nodded. I couldn't believe it. He never said anything to us, and now, here he was, a month before we performed, off-book on one of the most difficult choral and orchestral pieces ever written. Not only did he have our parts memorized—all four and sometimes as many as ten when we broke into small factions—he also had the orchestra parts memorized, the children's choir, the organ, the chamber choir and the soloists. As the main conductor, he had to know it all. And, in his quiet, humble way, he did.

I realized that I had been holding my breath and I let it out slowly. My shoulders relaxed. I could do this. It wouldn't be perfect, but that didn't matter. Dr. A held up his hands and winked at us. The strings took up their bows and we held our scores flat before us. Dr. A counted in the orchestra and they began with a quiet tremor from the timpani. We entered the music. We didn't think about whether we were late or not. We didn't count our mistakes. We didn't stop singing. We didn't give up. Even when the orchestra kept tempo and we lagged behind them, even when they reached a full *fortissimo* and we drowned in their sound, we did not give up. Dr. A cued us as if we were there, on time, with him. We raced to catch up, raced to make him proud, make the music proud.

When I saw him standing before us, waving his arms in that controlled but artful way, no score in sight, I felt a deep reverence enter the space among us—the space between Dr. A and the composer, the space between Dr. A and us, and, coming ever quicker, the space between me and the man who wrote this music, this music that demanded so much of all who dared to touch it.

On Good Friday 1962, a little over a month before the *War Requiem* premiere, Britten rests in bed in the Ipswich Nursing Home, recovering from an illness that had intensified while he and Pears toured in Canada. Rain patters against the window. Pears had visited earlier and brought paper, pens, books, and terrible news. Now, Britten takes out a sheet of paper and passes on what he has learned to his friend Princess Margaret of Hesse and the Rhine.

We've had the bitterest blow about the *War Requiem* at Coventry. The bloody Soviets have finally said 'no' to Galya singing—I haven't seen the note yet which I gather was polite and full of compliments to me, but we presume that the combination of Cathedral and West German (F. Dieskau) was too much. Curses on their beastly narrow politics! ...One had hoped to do a little.

He sets down the pen. What is he going to do? Who could possibly take Vishnevskaya's place? The music was written specifically for her voice, her talents. Additionally, he had wanted one singer from England, one from Germany, and one from Russia to sing together. Even now, almost twenty years after the Second World War ended, the world is still broken, nations still pitted against one another. How long does it take for change to happen? Real change? Sometimes it feels impossible. Britten leans back in the bed and the letter slides from his lap to the mattress edge. He closes his eyes and rests his hands on his chest. He waits and hopes that this feeling—despair—will pass.

As I AM reading *Letters from a Life*, I realize that the footnotes are moving into the future. The editors explain performances and tours that happen in the months following the performance of the *War Requiem*. Britten is already planning his next compositions, Pears his next performance tour. I have not thought ahead. Of course, Britten composed more works, of course, Pears performed other masterpieces. Of course.

And yet, it is difficult for me to understand. Everything I have been reading and thinking about has led me to this: learning about the first performance of *War Requiem*. Up until this point, the fact that I would reach the end had not seemed possible. Every time I listen to the music, I am reminded of different memories and emotions. Every time I open the books of letters, I grow closer to the men who wrote them. My education shifts and grows with each passing day. It is hard for me to grasp that it will end. I have known that Owen died in November of 1918, and that Britten conducted the premiere of the *War Requiem* in 1962, and that he then went on to compose more symphonies, choral works, operas, and sonatas. Owen's life ended, and Britten's time composing the *War Requiem* did, too.

How will I leave this material behind? For the first time, I understand that, eventually, I will reach an end. Someday—not tomorrow, not next week, or next month, but someday, someday soon, my journey with the *War Requiem* will end.

I do not want it to end. I do not know what my life will be like without it.

I turn on the first movement of the *War Requiem*. The beginning. I will not think of the end, just yet. I open the letters. I fall back into the world I have created around the *Requiem*.

THOUGH HE WORKS until eight at night with only one hour for lunch and one-quarter hour for tea, Owen is not unhappy in his camp because he received a new waterproof tent that he set in a field with long grasses and buttercups all around.

He spent two hours of his day seeing that the Rookies cleaned themselves well—especially their toes. Owen doesn't understand how people don't know how to bathe themselves properly, but these new conscripts from the Mills certainly don't, and he will follow orders, even if that means teaching a grown man how to scrub between his toes.

Just before the end of the day, Owen went to the medical tent to receive his typhoid vaccination. His arm already feels sore and he expects the fever and nausea to come on in a few hours. Before that happens, he wants to get a letter off to his mother and sort out a few poems. Owen enters his tent and pulls off his boots and socks, takes off his jacket and unbuttons his shirt. He sits down on the edge of his cot and pulls up a crate that he has fashioned into a makeshift desk. He had not planned to take out his books and papers while in camp, but he has received a letter from Edith Sitwell in London asking for more poems for their anthology. Scott Moncrieff, the Scottish soldier and writer, took an interest in Owen's poems after they met at Graves's wedding, and it was he who sent

Owen's poem "The Deranged" to Edith, Osbert, and Sacheverelle Sitwell.

Owen's mother sent him a cake a few days ago, and he takes out the last slice. He eats while spreading out a few of his poems on the crate. He looks over all he has written in the past few years and the shimmer of happiness he feels seems to match the sweetness of the cake on his tongue. From dirty toes in the morning to vanilla cake at night, his days are strange, but they are days, and he is thankful for them.

I READ A letter that Owen wrote to his sister Mary on May 29, 1918 in honor of her birthday. At the beginning he tells her he has swum in the afternoon and written a poem just before beginning his letter to her. Owen writes that he believes his poetry is much better than it was last year—so much so, that he takes one of the poems away from the beginning of the list as he adds a new one to the end. This, he explains, is why he feels no haste toward publication. His talent is just now developing, and he wants to give his poetry time to come into its own.

Owen writes to his sister that he wishes she had a calling, like writing is for him. He suggests music, painting, gardening, nursing, and embroidery. "Chiefly for your own benefit I am saying this," he says, "to give you some tie to Mother Earth. I feel that a light wind of grief, to say nothing of a storm, might blow you off your innocent feet…My religion says it is better to design a church than sit and look at its design once a week."

Owen closes the letter, but then adds beneath his signature a new date, 4 June, and a note that reads: "Withheld this pending Board today, which passed me Fit. I go to Scarboro' tomorrow."

When I read these words, it is as if a heavy stone, a frozen stone, has been placed upon my heart. He is being sent back to war. Exactly five months from the day he added that note to the letter, he would be killed in battle.

BRITTEN PULLS INTO the parking lot at Coventry for his first rehearsal with the choir and orchestra. He has only a handful of hours with the musicians before the premiere. He turns off the car and Pears reaches for his hand. Britten takes a breath and looks at him. No words pass between them, but Britten knows that Pears can feel his clammy palm, can sense his pulse ticking fast beneath his skin. They get out of the car and Britten grabs the score from the backseat. They walk toward the entrance of the Cathedral. Before the doors, Britten pauses. Pears stops with a hand still on the door and looks at him with eyebrows raised as if to say, *Are you ready?*

Britten looks down at the score in his hands. He has been working on this composition consistently for over a year and a half, and now the moment has come. He believes in every single note and marking on the pages, but now he has to raise his arms, invite other musicians into the score, and give the music to the audience. He always feels a little nervous before a first rehearsal or first performance, but there is something different about this composition. Every note is stamped with his personal, pacifist beliefs. He has to bring those beliefs to life with the hundreds of other musicians who will perform with him in the coming days. The only thing he can do to make himself move forward is to believe that it will happen. He has to put faith in each person waiting for him in the cathedral.

He nods at Pears, who opens the door. The choir members are taking their seats and paging through their scores with pencils in hand. The cathedral stretches tall and gorgeous above him as he walks toward the musicians. He notices diamonds of rich wood on the ceiling and an enormous wall of bright stained glass on his right. With each step toward the front of the cathedral, he gains confidence. This is his life's work, and these musicians are here to help him realize that work.

When Britten reaches the front of the orchestra and choir, he sees that the music stand is too small to hold the score. He calls over one of the festival workers who leaves straightaway to find a piece of plywood to attach to the rostrum so that the score can be opened properly. Britten makes do with the current stand and sets down the music.

His agent has asked soprano Heather Harper to fill in for Vishnevskaya as the soprano soloist. By the time they premiere, she will have had only ten days with the score, but Britten knows that she is professional and precise from their time working together in his operas *Peter Grimes* and *The Turn of the Screw*. Before he begins rehearsal, he goes over to talk to her. He notices that she has covered her score with marks; she has no doubt been practicing nonstop since she first received the music. She looks at him with a smile, but with nervous eyes, and he assures her that she will do a lovely job. She asks him a few questions and marks his answers in her score.

After Harper takes her place, Britten looks around at the cathedral and listens to the hum of people talking, the flipping of pages, the tuning and last-minute practicing of the orchestra. He takes a deep breath and stands at his place before them all. Immediately, they quiet down.

As Britten leads the musicians through rehearsal, he turns his head to the side and tries to hear how the sound moves out through the cathedral. He calls Meredith Davies, the other conductor, up to the podium to take over. Britten leaves the front of the cathedral and walks backward down the middle aisle. He crosses his arms in front of him and stops moving in the center of the cathedral. He sees Pears looking back at him from the front pew. Britten shakes his head at him. The sound isn't right. It is as if all the music is coming out into the cathedral and getting scrambled. A moment of panic, then fury races through him. He looks up at the chorus, the instrumentalists, and Davies holding his arms outstretched toward them. He looks at Pears, looking at him. These musicians have worked hard to learn the music he wrote. Their faces gleam beneath the spotlights. They sing and play with so much focus and dedication. The choir sings the *Hosanna* in the *Sanctus* and he closes his eyes. *Sanctus, Sanctus, Sanctus. Holy, holy, holy.* He pictures Owen's face, the kind eyes that saw too much, the lips that breathed poetry before he went to sleep. The brass reverberates through him, and Britten feels as though wings are beating around his body. *Holy, holy, holy.*

Britten feels his chest swell with something that must be gratitude. He cannot worry about the acoustics. He has no control over that. All he can do is work with the musicians to create music that is as clear and precise as possible. They cannot make this piece perfect, but they can make it excellent.

He walks toward the sound. He holds up his hands and the musicians stop. He looks toward the person playing the crotales, the cymbals in the beginning of the movement. "You must sound like echoes from ages past," Britten says, and the instrumentalist nods. Britten raises his hands and they begin again.

I SIT DOWN at my kitchen table and my hands don't reach for the keyboard. They shake and I try to hold them still in my lap. The books of letters rest on either side of me, their covers closed. I look at them and I tell myself to open them and begin again, but my hands don't move. I stand up and walk back and forth in my cramped kitchen, one hand on my chest, the other pressing hard just below my ribs. I try to quiet my breathing, which is coming faster and faster. I look up to the slanted ceiling with blurring eyes. I make myself stop pacing. What am I feeling?

I close my eyes and feel the tears fall cool across my face. My heart races beneath my hand.

I am afraid. I am so afraid.

I wish I could talk to Britten. I would ask him, how do you know you're writing the correct notes? How do you let go of something that has been inside of you for so long? Did you ever feel afraid to finish? Did you ever let yourself glance ahead and see a wide, terrifying blank? I would tell him that I feel as though I'm about to parachute out of a plane. I know I will land and that the ride down will be beautiful, but I am caught between the roar of the engine and the sharp wind whipping my hair and I am gripping the metal bars of the plane and I cannot do it. I cannot let myself fall.

I turn around to look at the wall I have dedicated to Owen and Britten. I see their portraits, I see a picture of Coventry's ruins, a photograph of Sassoon with just a hint of a smile in his full lips. I see lyrics of the *War Requiem*, the Latin translations, the Owen poems featured in the piece. I see Post-it notes scrawled with dates and titles of musical pieces. I see my friends' handwritten notes to me, encouraging me. And then I notice two long strips of paper that, for some reason,

I nailed to the wall instead of taped. They are almost hidden beneath so many images—I had forgotten they were there. They are words by Joan of Arc that I heard over and over in my religion classes growing up. They are words I forgot.

I am not afraid. I was born to do this.

I am not a musical genius like Britten. I am not as brave or as talented as Owen. I am just me, a young woman from Minnesota who loves music and who loves words. I have filled my home in Virginia with the spirits of these men and their friends and family. Their words course through me. With shaking hands, I reach up and touch their faces, I touch their poems and compositions.

I am not ready for the end, but the end always comes. I have to let myself fall, but I will not fall alone. I will fly tandem with ribbons of words and melodies soaring before and behind me.

I tell myself that I am not afraid. I open the book. I begin again.

Today, Owen lines up just outside of camp to practice revolver shooting. The Webley Mk IV issued to most of the British soldiers is a jumpy gun when fired and requires practice. It has been a while since he shot his revolver; a little over a kilogram, the Webley sits heavy in his hand. A man tugs on a pulley rigged to a rail of targets, and one advances toward Owen. He cocks the hammer back, lines up his sight, and shoots. The noise blasts around him and he holds the gun steady with both hands so that the barrel doesn't jump too much. He re-sights after the shot and fires again. Another pulley gets tugged and a different target comes toward Owen. He cocks the gun, shoots, and the metallic thunder and smoke from the gun explodes around him once again. After six shots, after the targets are shot through with his bullets, Owen presses the thumb catch and flicks the gun down to eject the spent cartridge shells. The gun rests in his hand, smoking, waiting for him to feed it more bullets. His superior nods at him from a few meters away and he loads six more bullets. Owen snaps the gun back into position. Even after so much time away from guns and bullets, his hands move around the gun like air. He could not forget how to load and fire a gun if he tried. He shoots one more round, ears ringing, hands tingling, and he doesn't miss a shot.

AT ST. OLAF, we stood outside the chapel in small clumps, straightening each other's stoles and gripping our scores in sweating hands. After months of rehearsing the *War Requiem*, it was time to sing the piece for the last time. We breathed as a group beneath the tower of chimes in the center of campus. We listened to the wind moving through them. Nobody spoke. Candice put her arms around me and I reached to hold her, too. When we pulled away from each other, we were left clasping hands. We looked at each other and smiled. After four years singing next to each other in choir, I knew her voice as well as my own.

When we began rehearsing the *War Requiem*, we had no idea what we were singing. Now, we knew every note, and we knew that we would represent each one with a full breath and as much understanding as we could manage. We knew we were singing something important. We prepared to open ourselves up to it.

Dr. A walked toward us from the chapel. From the look on his face, I could tell that he was ready to enter the music and he was ready to lead us there with him. He smiled and said, "It's time to go."

We lined up and put our scores inside the right sleeves of our robes. We knew our performance would not be perfect. With the *War Requiem*, perfection was impossible. But we would come as close as we could. We would lift our faces and follow Dr. A's hands. We would not look away from him once and we would let our voices be pulled from us like streams of light. In one long line, all one hundred of us approached the chapel. My cranberry robes swished about my ankles for the last time. I stared up at the sky, and though I did not pray much, I thanked God in that moment for bringing me to this choir, this music, and to this new person—myself—who was being changed by each note she sang.

FOR MANY DAYS, Owen had been worried about Sassoon, whom he knew was fighting on the front lines, and then, one morning in late July, he receives word that Sassoon had been mistaken for a German spy and had been shot in the head by a British sniper. Somehow, he is still alive.

Owen endures another round of inoculations, but throughout the fever and shaking, he can think only of his dear friend. Sassoon, who taught him so much about poetry and war, Sassoon whose recent book is a marvel and will surely change people's views of war, Sassoon who understood him as a soldier, a poet, and a friend. Owen lies on his back and stares at the ceiling of his tent. He is burning up and yet he can't stop shaking. He knows that the medic would tell him his shaking is a symptom of the inoculation, but he feels that his body responds only to his despair at his friend being injured, and at his fervent wish to be with him.

A few days later, Owen receives a letter from Sassoon. His injury must not be so bad, if he can already write. Owen reads the letter, full of joy at seeing the familiar swoop of his friend's handwriting. As he reads, he understands that Sassoon has been undone by war once again. There is no way he will go back now. When he finishes reading the letter, he folds it back into its envelope, so that he can send it along with his next letter to his mother. It will be safe with her. He wants every piece of writing by his friend to last.

Soon Owen will go for a medical inspection with twenty-one other soldiers in order to be declared fit for draft. They will be sent on as soon as the medics complete inspection. After days of work in the camp, after a year of recovering in the hospital, this motion to go back to war seems right. There are no other options. There were never other options. When Britain entered the war, a great wave of honor and responsibility swept up every young man. Owen had entered the current and it had led him here. He looks out of the tent toward the field of buttercups. It is August, the end of summer, and the flowers are losing their brightness now and starting to wilt. He clears his throat as if about to speak and turns to the paper with his own familiar hand slowly spreading across the page.

"I am glad," he writes to his mother on August 10, 1918, "That is

I am much gladder to be going out again than afraid. I shall be better able to cry my outcry, playing my part." He continues writing about the news of war and his work in the camp, but his mind orbits around other things, his friends, namely. Their faces float up before his mind's eye and they are so real, so vivid, Owen feels as though he could reach out and stroke the hair on their heads, touch a hand to their cheeks, kiss their foreheads. Mary, his mother, his brothers, Sassoon... "My mind is a cobweb of lines radiating to Shrewsbury, London, Hastings, Berwick, London, Shrewsbury, Berwick, Edinburgh, Portsmouth—"

He closes the letter with his initials and falls back on the cot. That night he dreams of another face—his own—collecting rainwater in the creases about his eyes. He is floating in a black river. Owen wakes with his arms outstretched, waiting for someone to save him.

ON THE NIGHT of the premiere, May 30, 1962, the cathedral is packed. People pay fifteen shillings for seats in the back, two guineas for seats in the front. From his place in a small room off the side of the stage, Britten can hear people talking and milling about, rustling the pages of the programs that contain the nine Owen poems featured in the music.

Britten does not need to review the score on the night of the premiere. Every note he wrote has become a part of him. He will never forget the notes of the *War Requiem*.

Britten will conduct the tenor and baritone soloists with the chamber orchestra, and two other conductors, Meredith Davies and John Strickson, will lead the other sections. Britten folds his hands. Davies will do a wonderful job conducting the chorus, which is made up of multiple choirs from the Coventry Diocese. Each time the choirs met to rehearse, they had new challenges in front of them, the movements of the composition arriving in the mail for them like a magazine serial. It really is a wonder they have learned such difficult music in so short a time; the majority of the chorus are not professional singers. While the choir is not technically perfect, they have a heart about them that Britten feels certain will carry the notes.

People take their seats in the cathedral. If he closes his eyes, he can almost hear the hum of all their beating hearts. The BBC broadcasters motion for the musicians to come onstage; the announcer must have finished his introduction already. Britten shakes his head at them, for many in the audience still talk and mill about. The BBC waits, even though their radio waves now play silence. Britten straightens his tuxedo and breathes deeply. The last few people in the audience sit down and he nods at the man from the BBC.

The Coventry Festival Chorus, the City of Birmingham Symphony Orchestra, and the Melos Ensemble begin to stream onstage in lines and the audience starts applauding. He watches Pears and Fischer-Dieskau and Harper walk onstage. He cannot see the choir boys from the Holy Trinity Church in Leamington and the Holy Trinity Church in Stratford-upon-Avon and their director in the balcony, but he knows that they are there and they are ready. He takes a breath. He nods at Davies, who stands beside him, and Britten shakes his hand. Then Davies enters the scene, and Britten watches his back as he walks into the spotlight. The final piece to put in place is himself. They wait for him.

Before he lets himself think too much about all that will happen in the next hour and a half, Britten steps onto the stage and walks toward his place at the side with the chamber orchestra. As soon as he starts walking, he ceases hearing the applause. All he can see is the blur of the musicians' black and white attire, the gleaming wood of the instruments, the shining reflections of light off the polished brass. When Britten reaches his place, his surroundings snap into focus. He hears the applause patter off into silence. He waits for a moment and breathes. Then he looks at Davies and nods. Davies raises his baton with one hand before the chorus and orchestra. Davies gives them one beat. The gong and piano sound, and the *War Requiem* begins.

OWEN'S FEET BEGIN turning black and blue. Trench feet. Owen's assigned soldier-servant, Jones, thinks that it is the old frostbite playing jokes on him. Maybe it was the rainwater that had filled his tent a few weeks ago.

Whatever caused it, Owen can't walk. Every step feels like walking on pieces of glass. If he walks more than a few feet, nausea overtakes him and he has to put his head down and remind himself to breathe.

He sleeps in his tent all day. At night, he has Jones bring him some paper and a pen. He misses his mother so much. He wishes she could be here with him, gently washing his feet and drying them, holding his hand as she did when he was little boy and feeling ill.

He writes to his mother: "There is nothing in heaven or earth like you, and that is why I can't write a poem for you...Eat, Drink, and Be Merry, for tomorrow we live, and the day after tomorrow live, live, live. Even in Scarborough I must live; though I feel dead to all these people...I am thinking wildly and crying a little for only you to hear."

When Britten is not conducting the chamber orchestra, he rests with his head slightly down and feels the vibrations of the hundreds of voices and instruments move through him. His chest quakes in the middle of all the sound. He swears he can see his fingers shake with each pulse of the timpani. Britten feels wings beating around him. It is as if each musician's soul and each soldier's soul of which they sing has flown out into the air around them. He lets himself fall into the trance of the music. He does not need to look at the score. He knows each entrance as well as he knows the lines on his lover's face. The violins of the main orchestra play their last notes of the section, and Britten brings in the harp, that glint of irrepressible hope Owen never lost, then the cello, that sturdy reminder that pushes the melody forward.

He holds up a hand to Pears and catches his voice in his palm. "What passing bells for these who die as cattle?" Pears sings in a clear voice. Britten directs the chamber orchestra with sharp turns of his hands and feels the instruments create a cradle for Pears's voice. They have locked into one another's sound, they have found the balance. At the end of this solo section, he follows Pears's lead for the *ritardando* and gives the violins the appropriate tempo for the last few measures of the section. At the moment he draws his hand closed, Davies's opens and the chimes ring out, creating the next space in which the choir enters, singing *Kyrie eleison, Lord have mercy upon them.*

WE TURNED OUR pages as quietly as possible and we never stopped watching Dr. A. I listened to the snare drum beat out march after march. The brass flew above our voices like those bugle calls of war were meant to do. The violins played their mournful intervals. The timpani crashed and rumbled beneath us, reverberations from far-off blasts. We sang and sang until our abdomens tightened from all our breathing and until our throats grew dry and cracked, and still we sang. The music surrounded us like giant hands and I felt lifted up in the midst of it all. Although I could not hear my own voice, I knew I was singing. I kept on. I barely looked at my score.

ON SEPTEMBER 15, 1918, Owen rejoins the 2nd Manchesters at Corbie, France. He watches the Manchesters march in and he recognizes two young men instantly as they walk by. They were almost the only survivors of the ranks he had fought with previously.

Owen and the 2nd Manchesters do not fight at the front yet, but they move closer every day, and the shells still blast nearby.

Owen writes to Sassoon. "This is what shells scream at me every time: Haven't you got the wits to keep out of this? … P.S. my Mother's address is Mahim Monkmoor Rd. Shrewsbury. I know you would try to see her, if————I failed to see her again."

He seals the envelope and looks through his trunk at the papers and backs of envelopes that he has covered with his poetry. He sent many drafts home to his mother for safe-keeping and others have found homes in magazines, but there are many that he carries with him as he moves closer to the front. How many more poems will he write in his lifetime? When the war ends—if he survives—to what will he turn his attention? He looks down at the neatly stacked drafts, so many words he wants to think about and write over again. As he evolves, the words must too. Will these poems ever be finished? Are these the only poems he will leave to his name?

IN THE LAST movement, Britten, the tenor and baritone, and the chamber orchestra emerge from the explosive sound of the main orchestra like a fine mist of smoke and debris settling after a barrage. In this final movement, the soloists sing one of Owen's last poems, "Strange Meeting," about two enemy soldiers meeting in the afterlife. Pears's voice is the first to creep into this eerie, deadened space. He sings so quietly: "It seems that out of battle I escaped, down some profound dull tunnel..." Britten watches Pears's face. Pears looks ghostly, angelic, as if he really were the dead soldier about whom he sings.

Then, Dietrich Fischer-Dieskau enters the music and sings, "Whatever hope is yours, was my life also...The pity of war." When Fischer-Dieskau sings the word "pity," his voice cracks and in that crack, Britten can hear all the pain Fischer-Dieskau has endured—his own time as a German prisoner of war in Italy, the forced starvation and death of his brother, the bombing of his mother's home—begin to escape. Britten looks into Fischer-Dieskau's eyes and they glisten in the light. Britten can see that the ghosts of Fischer-Dieskau's dead friends and family are rising before his eyes.

"Let us sleep now," Fischer-Dieskau sings.

The organ enters with the boys' choir, those voices of so many angels. Then the main chorus comes in quietly with the soprano soloist and the orchestra. All of the voices swell like a river from F# minor to F major, to a sound of resolution. Britten stands with his arms outstretched and the music flows over him like sun-warmed water.

Every group decrescendos and the pattern repeats itself, softer this time, until everything fades to nothing. In that silence, the chimes ring out. Then, as soft as a whisper, a small flutter of wings, the choir sings, *Requiescant in pace. Let them rest in peace. Amen.*

Then all of the sound disappears. Britten feels his heartbeat, slow and steady, move through his chest, his hands, his fingertips. He can feel everyone in the room breathing in the heavy stillness. As he requested in the program, no one applauds. Minutes pass.

Finally, Davies looks at him and Britten returns the stare, but he cannot move. He feels as though he will never move. It is only when

Davies begins slowly walking off the stage, that Britten can put one foot in front of the other and make his way out of the cathedral.

AT FIVE IN the morning on October 10, 1918, Owen leads his Company outside to walk around their camp. The stars shine above them, and a mysterious, thin mist swirls and gathers around their ankles. They walk the perimeter, searching the horizon, warming up their bodies for the day of work ahead. Owen feels suspended in between the earth and sky, mist above him in the form of starlight, mist below him, rising from the ground. He lets the wide open horizon enter his mind. He walks as if floating. He forgets about time, the war, his family, his writing. He is simply a small being walking between earth and sky.

When dawn breaks, he stops, shocked at the sudden onrush of light after so much shimmering darkness. Another day begins. He wakes up to himself and walks toward the tents where the new lads from Scarborough sleep after showing up at camp in the middle of the night. They left their rations ten miles away, and somehow Owen must find food enough to feed them all. These new additions, along with his own Company, have been murmuring about talks of peace for days. He is under orders to make the whispers of peace cease. Even though he does believe that peace is coming, Owen and the rest must march ahead as though war will always be upon them.

WHEN WE SANG the final "Amen" of the *War Requiem* at St. Olaf, I felt a warmth move through my body. I would never sing with my Chapel Choir again, but the last note I sang was whispered, awe-filled, and full of thanks. When we faded into silence, not one person moved. We stood still, our mouths still open from our last note, and waited for the applause. It didn't come. Dr. A stood before us, one hand still resting in that final closed note. His eyes were closed, his head bowed. I looked at him, and the audience sitting still beyond him, and the stained glass shining in the light above our heads. In that moment, I stood in the middle of a prayer.

Two full minutes and thirty seconds later, the audience burst into applause. The sound was deafening and did not stop for minutes.

IT IS DIFFICULT for Owen to sense the passing of time accurately. The space between the initial sound of a shell being released and the huge explosion of its impact seems like many minutes, and the moment that a plane's engine goes quiet while it opens its belly and drops a bomb, seems like hours.

On Saturday, October 19, 1918, he leaves the damp tent for a place he calls the "False Floor Dug Out" in Bohain and Bussigny, areas of fighting still far back from the front line. This dugout goes down about fifty feet, but a false floor has been placed five feet below the surrounding ground. When Owen stands upon the false floor, he imagines the depth of open space below him, and a shudder goes through him. The world will swallow them all.

Owen and the other men in his Company have Thursday's *Times* and they read together that the Dual Monarchy of Austria and Hungary will soon enter the process of dissolution. Even this news from the paper is not certain, and the horizon continues to thunder with sounds of heavy artillery, mortars, and mines exploding. Owen feels the ever-present rumble of war move through him. He wonders how and when all of this will end. When he closes his eyes and looks up toward the sky, he senses his mother's prayers shrouding him like armor, light and warm as sunlight.

A FEW DAYS after the premiere, Britten receives a letter from Wilfred Owen's brother, Harold, who had written to him the day after he heard the first performance on the radio. He opens the letter and reads the words of Owen's brother: "I found your magnificent mass most disturbing, which I feel certain was your intention when creating this—if I may say so— superb music. It is a wonderful thought for me to possess that Wilfred's poetry will for ever be a part of this great work." Britten sets the letter down on the table and places a hand atop the paper. He stands there with his eyes closed and does not move for many minutes.

After Britten replies to Harold Owen with sincere thanks, he receives another letter from him about a month later. He opens the letter while he sits outside with his cup of tea. The *War Requiem* still courses through his mind, but it decrescendos a little bit each day. He knows that when he reads Harold Owen's letter, the melodies will come crashing through him once again. He unfolds the letter. He reads:

> May I say at once what intense pleasure it will give me to send you a picture of Wilfred that I really like myself. I have one I especially think is W. as I remember him best. It was taken in his student days—1912—I only discovered it five years ago when I was going through my sister Mary's papers after her death…The loveliness of the whole Requiem still absorbs my mind; but what really haunts me are those beautiful final passages where Pears and Fischer-Dieskau, with such glorious singing, bring out the perfection of 'Strange Meeting'…

The melodies rush into Britten again and he feels the power and the pain behind the voices. In that moment, and in every moment where he revisits the *War Requiem*, he feels as if he knows Wilfred Owen. Now, to have his brother writing letters to him—it is unearthly, miraculous.

Some months later, he receives the photograph in the mail, and, after that, a manuscript of a draft of "Anthem for Doomed Youth." In the photograph, Owen's hair is shining in the sun. His face is soft and free of worry. It is the young poet as he was when he fell in love with words. Britten cannot stop looking at the photo. He feels as though he has met Owen in another life. He would have liked to talk to him and say that he hoped the music suited his words: *the pity of war.*

The manuscript is full of crossed out words, strongly written exclamation and question marks, and a few ink spots in the lower right hand corner. Britten wonders where Owen was when he wrote these words. He hopes that it was somewhere warm, and dry, and light, and that, for a moment, he could not feel war's touch.

It is a warm April evening in the Roanoke Valley. I have opened the door to my balcony and golden light spills across the tiled floors and walls of my little cottage. I can hear birds singing to one another, and somewhere, a plane roars above me in the sky.

This evening, I read the last of Owen's letters at my kitchen table. Throughout the final weeks of his life, he kept telling his mother in the letters that he was not heading to the Line, that he was safe, and would be for a while. He warned her not to think of him as in danger if he wrote to her upon a Field Card. He also told her that he needed brand new socks, not ones that had been darned or mended, and that he wanted a small pad of paper and some fruit and nuts.

When I read his last letter, I cannot help but smile. He describes his night on October 31, 1918, spent in a smoky cellar in a house near the Ors Canal in France. Friends surround him, laughing at jokes, peeling and cutting potatoes, chopping wood. Owen, writes:

> It is a great life. I am more oblivious than alas! yourself dear Mother, of the ghastly glimmering of the guns outside, & the hollow crashing of the shells.
>
> There is no danger down here, or if any, it will be well over before you read these lines.
>
> I hope you are as warm as I am; as serene in your room as I am here…Of this I am certain you could not be visited by a band of friends half so fine as surround me here.   Ever Wilfred x

Four days later, on November 4, 1918, Wilfred Owen is killed on the bank of the Sambre-Oise Canal.

I read in the final footnote of *The Collected Letters* that twenty-three other men were also killed that day, eighty-four were wounded, and eighteen went missing. Each one of the men who died alongside Owen that day, and each one of the ten million soldiers and seven million civilians who died during World War I, had a life rich and full of sunlight.

One week after Owen was killed, World War I ended. Owen's mother received word of his death on Armistice Day.

When I finally close the book of Owen's letters, my throat feels tight, but I do not feel the heavy despair that I expected. Instead, I look up to Owen's portrait. One hundred years after he died, I have re-lived his life. Every time I lift my face toward the sun, I will know that I am feeling the same warmth that touched his face.

THE END OF the Decca album of the *War Requiem*, the album that I have now listened to more times than I can count, leads right from the final "Amen" of the *Libera Me* into recordings of rehearsals the day Decca recorded the composition. As soon as the final words of the choir fade away, the next track plays, and I hear frantic violins and cellos and horns practicing their parts all at once. After a few seconds, I hear a clap and Britten's voice saying, "Please, quiet please," and the orchestra quiets down. He gives them corrective notes about tempo, pronunciation, and how much direction they can expect from him. He says things like, "Timpani, please, can you make a quicker diminuendo after the accent on the A?...Violins, we've gotten a bit too loud now at figure three... it needs *pianissimo* playing, but playing...Chorus, I have to admit the composer was right, *mezzo forte* is too much, so go back to *piano*, but it must be clear." After he says this, I can hear the chorus laugh quietly.

I love listening to this recording of the *War Requiem*, because when I hear those final performance notes fade and the rehearsal begin, I understand that the end of the *War Requiem* never truly comes. Out there, somewhere, an orchestra is tuning up, a young woman is clearing her throat and gripping her score. A conductor taps his baton on the music stand and the musicians quiet. They hold wonder and awe and determination inside of them. They know it will be difficult. They know it will be impossible to reach perfection. Still, they take a breath. Still, they begin.

NOTES

While many of the details surrounding the lives of Wilfred Owen and Benjamin Britten have been imagined in an attempt to achieve a greater, more felt truth, the heart of each scene comes from fact. For these facts, I am indebted to the work of many others who care deeply about these men. In particular, I have relied on two books of letters, *Letters from a Life: The Selected Letters of Benjamin Britten*, edited by Donald Mitchell, Philip Reed, and Mervyn Cooke, and *Wilfred Owen: Collected Letters*, edited by Harold Owen and John Bell. These books have grown dear to me, and the care with which the collections were put together has been an inspiration and comfort as I turned their pages again and again.

I am also thankful to have had access to Neil Powell's *Benjamin Britten: A Life for Music,* "In Parenthesis," a poem written by another World War I soldier and artist named David Jones; and the online resources of The Wilfred Owen Association and The Britten-Pears Foundation.

Of course, I am indebted to the score of the *War Requiem*, published by Boosey & Hawkes, and to the 1963 Decca Recording featuring Dietrich Fischer-Dieskau, Peter Pears, and Galina Vishnevskaya.

The following works served as touchstones as I discovered how to structure this book: Ian Bostridge's Schubert's *Winter Journey: Anatomy of an Obsession;* David Jones's *In Parenthesis: Seinnyessit e Gledyf Ym Penn Mameu;* Rebecca Mead's *My Life in Middlemarch;* Maggie Nelson's *The Argonauts;* and Paisley Rekdal's *Intimate: An American Family Photo Album.*

BIBLIOGRAPHY

"Aldborough Roman Site." *English Heritage*, www.english-heritage.org.uk/visit/places/ aldborough-roman-site. 2015.
"Benjamin Britten's War Requiem." *For One Night Only*, Season 1, Episode 1, British Broadcasting Company, 18 May 1999.
Blythe, Alan. "Dietrich Fischer-Dieskau obituary." *The Guardian*, 18 May 2012, www.theguardian.com/music/2012/may/18/dietrich-fischer-dieskau. 2015.
Britten, Benjamin. *Letters from a Life: the Selected Letters and Diaries of Benjamin Britten 1913-1976.* Edited by Donald Mitchel et al., Faber and Faber, 1991.
Britten, Benjamin. *War Requiem*, Op. 66. Decca, 1963.
Britten, Benjamin. *War Requiem*, Op. 66. Decca, 2013.

Britten, Benjamin, Imogen Holst, and Wilfred Owen. *War Requiem*. Op. 66. London, New York: Boosey & Hawkes, 1963.

Britten-Pears Foundation, The Britten-Pears Foundation, brittenpears.org. 2015.

Duffy, Michael. "Weapons of War—Pistols." *Weapons of War*, www.firstworldwar.com/weaponry/pistols. 2015.

Elliot, Graham. *Benjamin Britten: The Spiritual Dimension*. Oxford University Press, 2016.

Fetthauer, Sophie. "Music in the Bergen-Belsen DP Camp." *Music and the Holocaust*, www.holocaustmusic.ort.org/memory/dp-camps/belsen-dp-camp. 2019.

Grogan, Christopher. "Daughter of the renaissance." *The Guardian*, 17 October 2007, www.theguardian.com/music/2007/oct/17/classicalmusicandopera. 2015.

Hibberd, Dominic. *Wilfred Owen: A New Biography*. Ivan R. Dee, 2003.

"Interactive World War I Timeline." *The National WWI Museum and Memorial*, www.theworldwar.org/explore/interactive-wwi-timeline. 2015.

Kildea, Paul. Benjamin Britten: *A Life in the Twentieth Century*. Penguin Books, 2014.

Lewis, Daniel. "Dietrich Fischer-Dieskau, Lyrical and Powerful Baritone, Dies at 86." *The New York Times*, 18 May 2012, www.nytimes.com/2012/05/19/arts/music/dietrich-fischer-dieskau-german-baritone-dies-at-86.html. 2015.

Mason, Colin. "From the Archive: 31 May 1962: Premiere of Benjamin Britten's War Requiem." *The Guardian*, 31 May 2012, www.theguardian.com/theguardian/2012/may/31/1962-benjamin-britten-war-requiem. 2015.

Miller, M. Geoffrey. *The WWI Diagnosis and Treatment of Typhoid Fever*, www.vlib.us/medical/osler.htm. 2015.

Olusoga, David. "Black soldiers were expendable--then forgettable." *The Guardian*, 11 November 2018, www.theguardian.com/world/2018/nov/11/david-olusoga-black-soldiers-first-world-war-expendable. 2019.

"Our History." *Coventry Cathedral*, www.coventrycathedral.org.uk/wpsite/our-history. 2015.

Owen, Harold. *Journey From Obscurity: Wilfred Owen, 1893-1918*. Oxford University Press, 1963-1965.

Owen, Wilfred. *The Collected Poems of Wilfred Owen*. Chatto & Windus, 1963.

Owen, Wilfred. *Collected Letters of Wilfred Owen*. Edited by Harold Owen and John Bell, Oxford University Press, 1967.

"Poetry Manuscripts of Wilfred Owen." *British Library*, www.bl.uk/collection-items/the-poetry-manuscripts-of-wilfred-owen. 2015.

Potter, Tully. "Galina Vishnevsakay obituary." *The Guardian*, 11 December 2012, www.theguardian.com/music/2012/dec/11/galina-vishnevskaya. 2015.

Powell, Neil. *Benjamin Britten: A Life for Music*. Griffin, 2014.

Richards, Anthony. "Letter Censorship on the Front Line." *The Telegraph*, Telegraph Media Group, 30 May 2014, www.telegraph.co.uk/history/world-war-one/inside-first-world-war/part-ten/10863689/why-first-world-war-letters-censored.html. 2015.

"Rosamund Strode." *The Telegraph*, 31 March 2010, www.telegraph.co.uk/news/obituaries/culture-obituaries/music-obituaries/7542193/Rosamund-Strode.html. 2015.

Rowe, Dilys. "From the Archive: 5 September 1960: Imogen Holst: business-like visionary." *The Guardian*, 5 September 2015, www.theguardian.com/music/2015/sep/05/imogen-holst-composer-conductor-interview. 2015.

Russell, Steve. "Tom Hiddleston and Dumbledore have visited this shop--have you?" *East Anglican Daily Times*, 19 January 2019, www.eadt.co.uk/ea-life/benjamin-britten-customer-of-aldeburgh-bookshop-1-5858231. 2019.

Sassoon, Siegfried. "Sassoon Journals." *Cambridge Digital Library*, University of Cambridge, 2015, www.cudl.lib.cam.ac.uk/collections/sassoon/1. 2015.

Sassoon, Siegfried. *Siegfried Sassoon Diaries, 1915-1918*. Edited by Rupert Hart-Davis, Faber and Faber, 1983.

Sitwell, Edith. *Edith Sitwell, Selected Letters 1919-1964*. Edited by John Lehmann and Derek Parker, The Vanguard Press, 1970.

The United States Holocaust Memorial Museum, The United States Holocaust Memorial Museum, ushmm.org. 2019.

The Wilfred Owen Association, www.wilfredowen.org.uk. 2015.

"Timeline of World War II." *Public Broadcasting Service*, September 2007, www.pbs.org/thewar/at_war_timeline_1939.htm. 2015.

"War Poets Collection." Edinburgh Napier University, www.napier.ac.uk/about-us/our-location/our-campuses/special-collections/war-poets-collection. 2015.

"War Requiem, Op. 66 (1961)." *Boosey & Hawkes*, www.boosey.com/cr/music/Benjamin-Britten-War-Requiem/15495. 2015.

"War Requiem." *Britten-Pears Foundation*, www.warrequiem.org. 2015.

"War Requiem Text." *California Institute of Technology*, www.its.caltech.edu/~tan/Britten/reqtext.html. 2015.

"Wilfred Owen." *Poetry Foundation*, www.poetryfoundation.org/poets/wilfred-owen. 2015.

Winter, Jay, editor. *Cambridge History of the First World War. Vol. 3*, Cambridge University Press, 2014.

World War One, British Broadcasting Corporation, www.bbc.co.uk/programmes/p01nb93y. 2015.

ACKNOWLEDGMENTS

I am overcome with gratitude at reaching this page. It would not have been possible without the support and love of so many, and it is now my impossible and joyful task to convey my unending thanks.

First, to Rebecca Brown, for selecting my manuscript and for your kind words about my work. Thank you.

To Katherine Agyemaa Agard. I am so happy to have my book come into this world alongside yours. Thank you for your fellowship.

Thank you to everyone at Essay Press. It has been an honor to work with you. Thank you to Kate Colby for your careful and insightful edits—the book is more itself because of you. Thank you to Travis Sharp for your support, your answers to my constant questions, and your beautiful design. Thanks to Mary-Kim Arnold for a fortifying, laughter-filled conversation early in the process.

To the editors who have given my work a home as I've been starting my career: Phong Nguyen and the team at *Pleiades*, Tricia Currans-Sheehan at *The Briar Cliff Review*, Sarah Pape at *Watershed Review*, Nina Correa-White at *Barely South Review*, and Henriette Lazaridis at *The Drum*. Thank you for your support. Thank you to Mike Good at *Coal Hill Review* for publishing an excerpt of this book and to Dinty Moore at *Brevity*'s Nonfiction Blog.

Thank you to Alexander Weinstein and everyone at the Martha's Vineyard Institute of Creative Writing. The week I spent there was transformative and has given me the courage to step into this moment.

I started this book during my MFA at Hollins University. That program and its people are so nurturing, giving, and fun. It was the perfect place to do some deep growing as an artist and person. Thank you to the Moody cafeteria staff, especially Paula Jones, for feeding my body and caring for my spirit. Thank you to Laura Jane Ramsburg and Janet Carty at the Eleanor D. Wilson Museum. Thanks to Jeanne Larson. To Elise Schweitzer.

Thank you to all of my Hollins classmates and teachers for walking alongside me, especially my Brave Little Band: Elisabeth Booze, Elizabeth Caldwell, Whitney Watson, and Richard Dillard. This book—and I—would not be the same without you. Thank you for the laughter and constant encouragement. There's no one with whom I'd rather get lost in a time warp. I love you all.

Thank you to Carrie Brown, my inspiration in writing and in life. Your generosity and your belief in me has meant the world. Thank you.

Thank you to my teachers at St. Olaf. To Wendell Arneson, for teaching me to paint and to trust myself as an artist. To Jennifer Kwon Dobbs, for encouraging me to follow my instincts. To Ben Percy. For saying yes and saying yes again. You have encouraged and supported me at every turn. These two words do not seem adequate in the face of all you have done for me, but here they are: Thank you.

To Jason Wallestad, my high school writing teacher turned friend. Every exclamation point in this book was written with you in mind.

To Spencer Miller. Thank you for your friendship, for reading this manuscript, and for checking my musical facts. Any errors in the book are entirely my own.

Thank you to my music teachers and conductors and the musicians in my life. Nancy Stockhaus. Jere and Kristina Lantz. Margaret Eaves-Smith. Sigrid Johnson. Thank you to Christopher Aspaas for leading me to the *War Requiem* and to Candice Jones for holding my hand on the way there.

To Marissa Mazek and Elisabeth Booze, the best readers a writer could hope for. Thank you for your precise and incredibly helpful comments on the manuscript. The book is better because of it. Thanks, too, for your friendship. I am lucky to have you.

To my dear friends and colleagues who have helped me more than they know: Amy Stockhaus. Elin Lantz Lesser and Andy Lesser. Annemarie Hittler. Mike Geerdes. Rorie Morrison. Tamsen Hutton. Maureen Gullen. Tucker and Rachael Hurrelbrink. Jordynne Rogers. Chris Grathwol. Connor and Clare Johnson. Forrest Cyr. Anna Miller. Alison Van Heel. B and Erin Hart. Emma Bohmann. Martha Park. Natasha Oladokun. Jose Richard Aviles. Max Johnson. Katie Belanger. Nan Onkka. Maura Brew. Tom Bakken. Emily Gasperlin.

To my in-laws. Tom and Pam, thank you for welcoming me into your family and for raising your son to be the perfect partner for me. Thanks to Danny and Morgan, Tipper and Alexandria, and to Camille/Sue. Your love and support has meant so much. To Grandpa Paul, Grandpa Gil, and Grammie. We miss you.

To the Mendosa crew, my family as much as any. Thank you to Gram Cracker and Gramps, my aunties and uncles and cousins. To my musical angels, Niecy Byrd Culbertson, Grandma Solveig, and Grandpala: this book is a conversation I wish I could have had with you.

To my brother, Max Preus. You inspire me and make me laugh more than anyone. I love you.

To my parents. You told me I could be a brain surgeon when I fainted at the sight of blood and an astronaut when I hated math. When I said I wanted to write a book, you never once doubted that I would. Thank you for your boundless belief in me. Thank you for bringing me to the bookstore every weekend when I was young and for filling our house with books. Thank you for the hours of phone conversations and for always showing up when I needed you: in Northfield and Virginia, in South Minneapolis and Bangkok.There will never be enough thank yous for the two of you. I love you.

To Michael and Cleo. Michael, exploring this world with you is the greatest gift of my life. Thank you for keeping me fed and full of laughter. Thank you for introducing me to new music and supplying the soundtrack to our love story. Thank you for your friendship and love, and for your steadfast belief in me and in us. I love you, Nugg.

KAIA SOLVEIG PREUS teaches writing in Minneapolis. She received her MFA from Hollins University and was a 2019 Author Fellow through the Martha's Vineyard Institute for Creative Writing. Her work has appeared in *The Briar Cliff Review*, *The Drum*, *Pleiades*, and elsewhere. She is currently at work on a novel and a collection of essays.

OTHER TITLES BY ESSAY PRESS

THE BODY: AN ESSAY / Jenny Boully

LETTERS FROM ABU GHRAIB / Joshua Casteel

A PRANK OF GEORGES / Thalia Field and Abigail Lang

GRIFFIN / Albert Goldbarth

ADORNO'S NOISE / Carla Harryman

I, AFTERLIFE: ESSAY IN MOURNING TIME / Kristen Prevallet

THE AGE OF VIRTUAL REPRODUCTION / Spring Ulmer

SINGING IN MAGNETIC HOOFBEAT / Will Alexander

THIS IS THE FUGITIVE / misha pam dick

IDEAL SUGGESTIONS: ESSAYS IN DIVINATORY POETICS / Selah Saterstrom

OF SPHERE / Karla Kelsey

LITANY FOR THE LONG MOMENT / Mary-Kim Arnold

OF COLOUR / Katherine Agyemaa Agard